DUNE

Frank Herbert

TECHNICAL DIRECTOR Maxwell Krohn
EDITORIAL DIRECTOR Justin Kestler
MANAGING EDITOR Ben Florman

SERIES EDITORS Boomie Aglietti, Justin Kestler
PRODUCTION Christian Lorentzen, Camille Murphy

WRITER Jason Clarke
EDITORS Justin Kestler, Karen Schrier

This edition published by Spark Publishing

Spark Publishing
A Division of SparkNotes LLC
120 Fifth Avenue, 8th Floor
New York, NY 10011

02 03 04 05 SN 9 8 7 6 5 4 3 2 1

Please send all comments and questions or report errors to
feedback@sparknotes.com.

Library of Congress information available upon request

Printed and bound in the United States

RRD-C

ISBN 1-58663-510-7

INTRODUCTION: STOPPING TO BUY SPARKNOTES ON A SNOWY EVENING

Whose words these are you *think* you know.
Your paper's due tomorrow, though;
We're glad to see you stopping here
To get some help before you go.

Lost your course? You'll find it here.
Face tests and essays without fear.
Between the words, good grades at stake:
Get great results throughout the year.

Once school bells caused your heart to quake
As teachers circled each mistake.
Use SparkNotes and no longer weep,
Ace every single test you take.

Yes, books are lovely, dark, and deep,
But only what you grasp you keep,
With hours to go before you sleep,
With hours to go before you sleep.

Contents

NOTE: This SparkNote uses the Ace Books edition of *Dune* published in 1990. Frank Herbert divides his novel into three books but does not include any chapter divisions. For ease of reference, this SparkNote divides the three books into smaller sections. A note at the beginning of each summary specifies which portion of the novel it covers.

CONTEXT

FRANK HERBERT WAS BORN in Tacoma, Washington, in 1920. After high school, he became a journalist and then served in the United States Navy during World War II. He then studied at the University of Washington and became a reporter and an editor for many West Coast newspapers, as well as a speechwriter for politicians. In 1969, Herbert became a full-time fiction writer, four years after the publication of his science-fiction classic, *Dune*.

During the 1950s and 1960s, Herbert published many stories in science fiction magazines, often in serial form. Unlike some of his fellow science-fiction writers, such as Isaac Asimov and Arthur C. Clarke, Herbert wrote stories that always involved social issues such as ecology. Herbert conceived the idea for *Dune* after studying a governmental project designed to halt the spread of sand dunes along the Oregon coastline. He imagined a world made entirely of sand and thus created the planet Arrakis.

Although *Dune* was accepted and read by the same circles who read Asimov and Clarke, Herbert's novel represented a new kind of science fiction. Asimov's and Clarke's works were original but stylistically plain—Asimov later claimed that in the early days of science fiction, all one needed was a futuristic idea. *Dune* combined the basics of science fiction's trademark futurism with strong literary and social ambitions. The novel boasted an elaborate epic plot and intricately developed characters with quasi-mystical powers such as telepathy and precognition. It also featured a bold ecological message.

Dune proved that literary science-fiction novels could be more than thinly veiled social satires, such as George Orwell's *1984* or Anthony Burgess's *A Clockwork Orange*. Like Tolkien's *Lord of the Rings* trilogy, *Dune* presents us with a self-contained world, complete with its own races, religions, politics, and geography. Herbert introduces this new world and then adds a fascinating and intricate story, with vivid characters and scenes bolstered by an underlying ecological message. *Dune* has become the central masterpiece of science fiction, just as *The Lord of the Rings* is to the genre of modern fantasy.

Plot Overview

D<small>UNE</small> is based on a complex imagined society set 8,000 years in the future. The setting is the year 10,191, and human beings have spread out and colonized planets throughout the universe. On the planet Caladan, Duke Leto of the House of Atreides is preparing to leave for his new position as the governor of Arrakis, a desert planet with valuable resources of melange, a spice drug that is extremely popular with wealthy people. Leto and his family, including his concubine, Jessica, and his son, Paul, suspect a trap by their rivals, the Harkonnens, led by Baron Harkonnen. Leto decides to settle on Arrakis because of its rich supplies of melange, despite warnings from his men, including his adviser, Thufir Hawat, and his master-of-arms, Gurney Halleck.

The Atreides arrive on Arrakis and the duke quickly moves to secure the planet from a Harkonnen attack. His main plan is to enlist the Fremen, the tough natives of the Arrakeen desert, as soldiers and advisers. Meanwhile, Paul's and Jessica's special abilities intrigue the Fremen. Jessica is a member of the Bene Gesserit, a school of quasi-mystical witches with strange powers. The Fremen believe that Jessica and her son are saviors who have come to lead them toward creating a lush paradise on the dry Arrakis.

Dr. Yueh, a member of the Atreides house, betrays them. The Harkonnens arrive and wipe most of the Atreides out by using Sardaukar, the super-soldiers of the emperor, who is secretly helping the Harkonnens. The traitor, Dr. Yueh, hands Duke Leto over to the baron, but in his guilt he helps Jessica and Paul escape. Dr. Yueh places a secret tooth in Duke Leto's mouth. Duke Leto dies by emitting poison gas from the secret tooth, in a failed attempt to kill the baron. Hawat and Halleck escape as well. Halleck joins the local smugglers while Hawat attempts to join the Fremen, but Hawat is captured by the Harkonnens. He then agrees to work for Baron Harkonnen as a Mentat, or thinker, while secretly plotting his revenge against the baron and against Jessica, who he thinks betrayed Duke Leto.

Dr. Kynes, a Fremen leader and planetary ecologist, orders the Fremen to find Jessica and Paul. The Fremen capture and then quickly accept Jessica and Paul as their destined leaders. Jessica

3

becomes their reverend mother, while Paul is recognized as something close to a religious prophet. Paul takes the name Muad'Dib, a religious title that means mouse. As he matures swiftly following his father's death, Paul discovers he has great powers above and beyond those of his mother. He can see into both the future and the distant past. His consumption of melange heightens his powers.

Two years pass. The baron, living on the Harkonnen home world, schemes to usurp the emperor, while grooming one of his own nephews, Feyd-Rautha, to take over the job. Meanwhile, on Arrakis, Paul has become very powerful and influential among the Fremen. He is both their secular and religious leader, like Kynes before him, but his powers are far greater than those of Kynes. He has a child with a Fremen woman, Chani, the daughter of Kynes, and his mother has given birth to Alia, Duke Leto's daughter. Paul teaches the Fremen to fight using a special style called the "weirding way" and using the advanced fighting techniques of the Bene Gesserit. One day, the Fremen discover that the baron has abandoned his aid to Rabban, the nephew he assigned to rule over Arrakis. Paul and the Fremen make plans to raid the Arrakeen capital now that Rabban is cut off from the baron's help.

Upon discovering the power of the Fremen, the emperor himself comes to Arrakis, along with his Sardaukar and the Harkonnens. The Fremen attack the emperor, quickly dismantling his spaceships while destroying the Sardaukar. In the battle, Alia kills Baron Harkonnen, and Paul's young son dies in a raid. Paul demands that the emperor step down; Paul asks to marry the emperor's daughter, Irulan, so that he may become the new emperor. Feyd-Rautha challenges Paul, citing the right of vengeance, and Paul kills him in a duel. Powerless now, the emperor agrees to Paul's demands, and Paul becomes the new emperor.

CHARACTER LIST

Paul Atreides The protagonist of *Dune*. Paul is the son of Duke Leto Atreides and is the heir to the House of the Atreides. At the beginning of the novel, Paul is fifteen years old. He has been trained from birth to fulfill the role of duke, and he is adept at combat and strategic thinking. Paul is also a quiet, thoughtful, and observant young man. Paul is not overly tall or muscular, but he is strong and quick. Among the Fremen, Paul has two names: Usul, which signifies strength, and Muad'Dib, the name of the desert mouse on Arrakis.

Jessica Paul's mother. Jessica is the concubine of Duke Leto Atreides. Though she acts like a wife to Leto and he has no other concubines, she is not married to Leto. Jessica is a member of the Bene Gesserit, a school that teaches and practices what many others think of as witchcraft. An orphan who never knew her parents, Jessica is tall and slender, with bronze-colored hair and green eyes.

Duke Leto Atreides Paul's father. Duke Leto Atreides is the head of the House of Atreides and the rightful ruler of Arrakis. The duke received Arrakis from the emperor in exchange for Leto's own planet of Caladan, which was given to the duke's mortal enemy, Baron Harkonnen. The duke is a wise, intelligent, and compassionate man, but he is ruthless when it comes to dealing with his enemies. He cares very much for his concubine, Jessica, and their son, Paul.

Baron Vladimir Harkonnen Leader of the House of Harkonnen. The baron is the mortal enemy of the House of Atreides. The baron is very fat, and his bulk is supported by electronic suspenders.

Thufir Hawat Duke Leto's master of assassins. Hawat is a well-known Mentat, or a person trained to act completely logically. He serves as Leto's main strategist and confidant. Hawat is old, having served three generations of Atreides. He has also trained Paul in combat and tactics.

Gurney Halleck Duke Leto's master of arms, or war master. Halleck is well trained in the use of numerous weapons, and he is particularly good at swordplay with the use of personal electronic body shields. He is fond of music and plays the baliset, a guitarlike instrument. He has trained Paul in the art of personal combat and is an old friend of the Atreides's.

Duncan Idaho Duke Leto's swordmaster. Duncan is a skilled warrior and a faithful servant of the duke and his family.

Reverend Mother Gaius Helen Mohiam Spiritual leader of the Bene Gesserit. Mohiam is old and serves as the emperor's truthsayer, a person who can tell the emperor whether someone is lying. Before he leaves for Arrakis, Mohiam puts Paul through a severe test of endurance.

Feyd-Rautha Harkonnen Nephew of Baron Harkonnen. Feyd-Rautha is the baron's first choice for an heir. The baron hopes to secure a vast amount of power for the Harkonnen family before Feyd-Rautha comes into his inheritance. Feyd-Rautha is nearly the same age as Paul.

Piter Baron Harkonnen's Mentat, a human trained to think logically, rationally, and mathematically to be the perfect adviser. Piter is ambitious and scheming, two emotional traits that are unusual and not desired in a Mentat.

Yueh   The Atreides's doctor. Yueh betrays the Atreides to the Harkonnens. His betrayal is particularly shocking because at this time, doctors of the Suk School are supposed to be heavily psychologically conditioned to never cause harm.

Stilgar   A leader of the Fremen, the native people of Arrakis who live in the desert. Stilgar is wise, experienced, and familiar with the legends and folklore of the Fremen.

Chani   Daughter of Liet-Kynes. Chani is one of the Fremen and has some of the skills of the Bene Gesserit. She is Paul's age and gives birth to his first child.

Emperor Shaddam IV The ruler of the Imperium. The emperor is arguably the most powerful man in the known universe, although he is often at the mercy of the Spacing Guild, which has a monopoly on space travel.

Liet-Kynes Planetologist for Arrakis, or an ecologist for planets. Unknown to the Harkonnens, Liet is also a member of the Fremen. He works with the Fremen to change Arrakis from a desert planet into a lush, green paradise.

Alia   Duke Leto and Jessica's daughter, and Paul's sister. Alia's mother took the "Water of Life" before she was born. Alia had a conscious awakening while in the womb and even at her birth was much more intelligent than most adults.

Shadout Mapes A Fremen and servant of the Atreides. Mapes is the first among the Fremen to test Jessica and discover that she is a Bene Gesserit. Mapes is later killed when Dr. Yueh betrays the Atreides to the Harkonnens.

Princess Irulan The emperor's eldest daughter. In the future, the princess writes several books about the Muad'Dib, who is a vastly important figure in the universe's history.

Esmar Tuek One of the head smugglers on Arrakis.

Staban Tuek The son of Esmar Tuek. Staban takes over for his father after his father's death.

Jamis One of the Fremen. Paul is forced to kill Jamis when the man challenges him to a duel to the death.

Harah Jamis's wife. Harah becomes Paul's servant after Paul kills her husband.

Count Fenring A servant and friend of the emperor's. The count is married to Lady Fenring. He is a very skilled man, particularly at killing others, and he was almost the Kwisatz Haderach.

Lady Fenring Married to Count Fenring. Lady Fenring is a member of the Bene Gesserit.

Rabban Harkonnen A nephew of Baron Harkonnen's. Before the novel begins, Rabban is the ruler of Arrakis. When the Atreides take over Arrakis, he must step down. However, Rabban rules Arrakis again after the Harkonnens seize back Arrakis.

ANALYSIS OF MAJOR CHARACTERS

PAUL ATREIDES

Paul Atreides carries the heaviest burden of all the characters in *Dune*—he is destined to change the course of the universe. From the start, we never get a sense that Paul is a typical fifteen-year-old boy. Like many other heroes, particularly in science fiction, Paul is "the One," a messiah-type character whose arrival people have been anticipating and expecting to bring about great change. Throughout the novel, Herbert makes cryptic references to the Kwisatz Haderach. Even in the very beginning, Reverend Mother Mohiam thinks that Paul may be the Kwisatz Haderach, which immediately establishes Paul's great significance as a character in the novel and as a figure within the universe of Dune.

Paul is different from the other "ones" in science fiction because of his steadfast resistance to his destiny and his concern about the consequences of power. Paul does not resist because he does not believe—he knows he is the Kwisatz Haderach. He resists because he can foresee the bloody war that will result throughout the universe following his rise to power. The Bene Gesserit have arranged for the advent of "the One" because they believe a war is the only way to diversify mankind's gene pool. Paul, however, wants to believe there is another way, one that does not cause so much suffering and death.

Paul weaves the path of his destiny by the way he attempts to resist it. For example, he does not want to kill Stilgar so that he can rise to power. Instead, he creates a new position within the Fremen hierarchy so that both Stilgar and himself can be leaders. Paul successfully becomes the religious leader of the Fremen. However, we always have a sense that he is fighting a losing battle with his destiny. Paul feels torn between his allegiances—to the House of Atreides, to the Bene Gesserit, and to the Fremen—and his role in the intergalactic politics of the Imperium and the Landsraad. At the end of Dune, although he helps the Fremen cause and protects the Atreides from destruction by the Harkonnen, Paul is nonetheless forever trapped in his role as the Muad'Dib. The simple happiness he craves with Chani remains unattainable.

JESSICA

Jessica is one of the most complicated characters in Dune. Like her son, she is the product of centuries of genetic breeding by the Bene Gesserit, an ancient school that teaches women how to develop superhuman mental and physical abilities. Jessica rebels against the school—she was instructed by the Bene Gesserit to bear a daughter, but she defied them and bore a son instead.

Jessica's character undergoes many changes. At the beginning of the novel, she is Duke Leto's concubine. The two are in love, but Leto will not marry her for political reasons. Leto knows that as long as he is unmarried, he has something to offer the other Great Houses. Despite her concubine status, both Leto and Jessica treat the relationship as a marriage, and Jessica is accustomed to her life as a wealthy duke's partner. Jessica's life changes once the Harkonnen kill Leto. She is forced to live in the harsh desert among the Fremen and use all her abilities to survive, including seducing her captors.

Jessica resigns her wifelike role and becomes a reverend mother, serving as a matriarchal figure to thousands of people. Jessica has been preparing for such a role by training as a Bene Gesserit from birth. Throughout the novel, however, she is often troubled by emotions that intercede with her loyalty to the Bene Gesserit. Most significantly, she regrets that she groomed Paul so well for the messianic role of Kwisatz Haderach. She realizes that she has robbed Paul of his innocence—he never has a childhood, a normal adulthood, or even the normal life as a duke's heir.

Like Paul, Jessica finds herself swept along by a subtle, yet firm current of time, leading inexorably to an unknown conclusion. Jessica is far more passive than Paul in receiving her fate because of her Bene Gesserit training. She accepts that her purpose in life is to work toward the collective goals of the Bene Gesserit. Only near the end of her exile on Arrakis does Jessica begin to see the infinite future possibilities that Paul has perceived all along.

BARON HARKONNEN

Baron Harkonnen appears infrequently in the novel, but he initiates an important sequence of events that changes the future of the universe. He deviously tries to murder the entire House of Atreides and hopes to control the empire by having a monopoly on spice. His grandiose plans even include becoming the new emperor. Ironically, the baron's plans drive Paul to become the leader of the Fremen and eventually leader of the universe. The baron is clearly marked as the novel's main antagonist from his very first appearance. He is ruthless, ambitious, cruel, and so fat that he requires antigravity devices to suspend his bulk.

The baron appears like an unrealistic caricature of a leader. On the surface, he is not very different from Duke Leto. Both men are ambitious and ruthless. Leto, however, genuinely cares about his own men and family and regrets many of the tactics he must use to protect them, such as poisoning his rivals and raiding their supplies. The baron seems to delight in the intricacies of political warfare, and his regard for his family extends no further than his beloved nephew Feyd-Rautha. The personalities of the leaders of the other houses fall somewhere between those of Leto and the baron.

The baron's villainous qualities are reflected in his sexual tastes, most notably his predatory preference for young boys. The novel suggests that the baron's affection for Feyd-Rautha stems largely from the nephew's youth, and we even see hints that the baron quietly lusts after Paul Atreides. Oddly enough, no other character in the novel takes a stance on the baron's perverse sexual tastes. The result is a disturbing ambiguity that leaves the moral boundaries of Herbert's imagined world unclear.

THEMES, MOTIFS & SYMBOLS

THEMES

Themes are the fundamental and often universal ideas explored in a literary work.

RELIGION AND POWER

Dune was one of the first science-fiction novels to address issues of religion. Many science-fiction authors considered religion an outdated institution that would eventually lose its direct control over society. Many writers assumed that the separation of church and state would only widen in the future. Frank Herbert had a different conception of the future. *Dune*'s universe employs a feudal government system that includes dukes and barons and in which religion has a very strong presence in everyday life and politics.

Religion's most obvious presence in *Dune* is in the Bene Gesserit. The Bene Gesserit are familiar with numerous religious texts, from the Orange Catholic Bible to more cryptic texts such as the Great Mysteries. These texts play a significant role in defining the Bene Gesserit conception of the world. The Missionaria Protectiva reveals that the Bene Gesserit frequently exploit religion to protect their own members. The Bene Gesserit use the Missionaria Protectiva to spread contrived legends and prophecies to developing worlds. Bene Gesserit can exploit these legends to earn the respect of the native inhabitants, who believe in the contrived legends.

The other important presence of religion in *Dune* involves control of the Fremen. Kynes's father is the first person to exploit religion as a method of rallying the Fremen to his cause—turning Arrakis from a desert planet to a lush, green world. Kynes and his father hope to bring paradise back to Arrakis through religion. Although Kynes wants to bring nature to Arrakis by making it a lush, green planet, his endeavor is contrary to nature because Arrakis is a naturally dry planet.

Religion represents a source of comfort and power throughout the novel. Paul pursues the same goals as Kynes, but he uses his religious power over the Fremen as their messiah to gain control of the entire Imperium. Paul possesses mystical abilities that go above and beyond a simple heightened awareness or intelligence, but his clever exploitation of religion is his most powerful advantage. Paul's adept manipulation of religion and the calculated use of legends contrived by the Bene Gesserit allow him to rise to the position of Emperor.

HUMAN CONTROL OVER ECOLOGY

To exist in the harsh desert climate of Arrakis, the Fremen must be keenly attune to ecological issues such as the availability of water, the proximity of giant sandworms, and unstable weather patters. The ecological issues in *Dune* extend beyond the mere necessities of daily life on Arrakis. Dr. Kynes, a prominent figure in the book, is an ecologist who hopes to transform the ecosystem of Arrakis from a desert to fertile, verdant splendor. The Fremen take up his cause, and Paul continues it after Kynes' death.

Altering Arrakis into a lush garden planet is performing the work of a higher power, reshaping the land to conform to the preference and needs of the Fremen. Yet no character in *Dune* ever questions whether it is morally right to change the climate of Arrakis. Changing the planet might kill the sandworms, which have an integral role in creating melange, an addictive drug used throughout the universe. Such a change in the ecosystem may also obliterate the muad'dib, the planet's beloved mice, and the source for Paul's new Fremen name. The Fremen are strong and powerful soldiers because they have trained in a harsh desert climate. The Fremen would not have the power to fight the Emperor's soldiers or change the climate of Arrakis if the environment were different.

Dune raises the question of whether humans should exercise their power to manipulate the environment, but lack of opposition from any character in the novel leaves no firm conclusion.

Herbert explores the moral question of manipulating nature with the issue of the gene pool in *Dune* as well. Paul is the Kwisatz Haderach, and his duty is to diversify the genetic makeup of the universe. Disturbing the natural genetic makeup may lead to a deadly holy war, or jihad. If human beings fight the natural order of life, whether through the environment or genetic codes, Herbert suggests, the results can be dire, even if the repercussions are not felt until far off in the future.

MOTIFS

> *Motifs are recurring structures, contrasts, or literary devices that can help to develop and inform the text's major themes.*

INHERITANCE AND NEPOTISM

It is ironic that *Dune*'s futuristic political system is based on the feudal system of the Middle Ages. Dukes and barons rule planets and sectors of space, and control passes down from one relative to the next in line. After the death of Duke Leto, Paul becomes the duke of Arrakis. Similarly, Baron Harkonnen plans to hand his power to his nephew Feyd-Rautha.

In the future society depicted in *Dune*, relatives inherit more than wealth. The "sins of the father" often pass to the children as well. The Atreides and the Harkonnens hold something called kanly against one another. Kanly is the right of vengeance. Any act performed by one against another can be lawfully reacted to in kind. The tenet of "an eye for an eye" applies to families and communities, not just to individuals. The Atreides and the Harkonnens spend their time raiding and killing one another, and each generation of Atreides and Harkonnens continues the cycle of vengeance and hatred.

Inheritance is important to both males and females for preserving knowledge and power. Paul's mother trains Paul in the skills of the Bene Gesserit. Jessica also passes her powers to her daughter, Alia. Similarly, Lady Fenring seduces Feyd-Rautha in order to carry his child as part of the Bene Gesserit breeding program. Paul worries that the Bene Gesserit's plan to reinvigorate the human gene pool can be accomplished only through jihad, a war that will spread across the universe. Birth and family lines are an integral aspect of relationships in *Dune* because they maintain tradition throughout thousands of years and thousands of worlds.

PRECOGNITION

One of the more distinctive aspects of *Dune*'s environment is the existence of precognition, or knowledge about events that have not yet occurred. The mystical ability of certain human beings to see into the future brings elements of fantasy into the novel.

Most of the characters with precognitive powers are members of Bene Gesserit or the Guild, but Paul develops this power beyond all others because of three factors: his genetic heritage, his Bene Gesserit and Mentat training, and his exposure to melange. Herbert never clearly describes the exact nature of Paul's powers, but given the improbable nature of some of Paul's predictions, his precognitive powers must work on a level beyond mere calculation.

Paul's precognition gives him control. By knowing the future, Paul can shape events in the present to attain the results he desires. Of all his powers, precognition is perhaps the most useful, as well as the most terrifying. Paul feels that his precognition is both a blessing and a curse. He is concerned about having too much control over people, such as the Fremen, but he also feels driven to achieve his ultimate goal of gaining control of the universe.

SYMBOLS

Symbols are objects, characters, figures, or colors used to represent abstract ideas or concepts.

MELANGE

Melange, the spice drug, is found in limited quantities on the planet Arrakis and mined by the Fremen. *Dune* was written in the early 1960s, when drug experimentation was beginning to enter the mainstream consciousness of America. *Dune* explores the concept of drugs as a way of opening "the doors of perception," a phrase penned by the poet William Blake that Aldous Huxley used as the title of a book about his experiments with hallucinogens. Consuming melange, which is highly addictive in large quantities, allows Paul to see through time and to perceive the future.

As a symbol, melange represents the untapped potential of human perception and brainpower. Melange allows Paul to achieve the greatest heights of his power and awareness. Melange is a costly crutch, however. Melange is highly addictive in large quantities, and Paul cannot survive without great quantities of it. The more he takes, the less the drug affects his awareness, and so he requires greater and more concentrated doses. Melange may open the "doors of perception," but its addictive force binds its users to the drug .

WATER

The Fremen refer to blood as "the body's water," suggesting that the Fremen view water as the blood of the environment. When Thufir Hawat agrees to join the Fremen, he enters the "bond of water," rather than a blood oath or blood brothers. People show their loyalty to each other by spitting or sharing water. Paul and Jessica, during their time with the Fremen, engage in countless rituals that involve water. For example, Paul accepts the water of Jamis's corpse after he kills him. After drinking this water, Paul is baptized into the culture of the Fremen, and he is reborn as a leader in their world. For the Fremen, water and life are one and the same.

SUMMARY & ANALYSIS

BOOK I

From the beginning through Paul's meeting with Dr. Yueh

SUMMARY

> *"A duke's son must know about poisons. . . . Here's a*
> *new one for you: the gom jabbar. It kills only animals."*
> (See QUOTATIONS, p. 54)

Dune begins on the planet Caladan, which is ruled by Duke Leto of the House of Atreides. The House of Atreides is one of the families that rules over the planets and planetary systems of the universe. Duke Leto's son, Paul, is in bed when his mother, Jessica, and Reverend Mother Mohiam check in on him. The old reverend mother mutters that Paul may be the Kwisatz Haderach, the one who brings about important changes in the universe. Reverend Mother Mohiam says that the next day, Paul will meet her gom jabbar, an instrument that poisons and kills instantly, unless he passes her test. To test whether Paul is human, the Reverend Mother Mohiam has him put his hand into a small box. The box brings great pain to Paul, but he knows that if he moves, the Reverend Mother Mohiam will stab him with the gom jabbar. He passes Mohiam's test, which means he is a human being and not an animal. He then discovers that Jessica took the same test long ago; the reverend mother was her teacher at the Bene Gesserit school. The two women reveal to Paul that something terrible will soon happen to the House of Atreides and that his father will die. The two women tell Paul that the duke's death will happen soon after the Atreides move to Arrakis, the desert planet, now ruled by the Atreides's mortal enemies, the Harkonnens.

On another planet, the fat Baron Harkonnen reveals his plot to his nephew Feyd-Rautha and his servant, Piter, a Mentat, a person who thinks using logic and no emotions. The baron has maneuvered the emperor, the leader of the universe, into giving the planet Arrakis to the Atreides in exchange for the planet Caladan. Though Arrakis is a desert planet and Caladan a lush one, this trade does not seem good for the baron; Arrakis is rich in melange, a drug and spice that is an addiction for millions of people throughout the galaxy. The baron has arranged this trade because he plans to kill Duke Leto and all his family once they are on Arrakis by using one of their own people to betray them. Piter trades barbs with his fat master as Feyd-Rautha looks on passively.

Back on the planet Caladan, the Reverend Mother Mohiam confronts Jessica and asks her why she did not have a girl, in accord with the Bene Gesserit's orders. Jessica replies that she did so because the duke wanted a son, an heir, very badly. The reverend mother chides her, saying that now there is no daughter to wed a Harkonnen, the rival house of the Atreides, and "[seal] the breach." Jessica and the reverend mother both know that the planet Arrakis is already lost and that the duke is as good as dead. They talk to Paul, and he recites a dream he had in which he met a girl who calls him Usul.

Later, Paul meets Thufir Hawat, the duke's main strategist, in the training room. Hawat warns Paul of the dangers he will face on Arrakis, but he tries to dispel Paul's fears that his father will be killed. He also mentions the Fremen, the native inhabitants of Arrakis. Hawat explains that the Fremen are a tough, resilient people, and they will have to be dealt with in some way by the Atreides. After Hawat leaves, Gurney Halleck, the duke's war master, appears and challenges Paul to a training duel. Paul fights well, but Halleck makes the battle difficult for him, since he knows that Paul may actually have to fight someone soon. Finally, Paul meets with Dr. Yueh, a doctor of the Atreides, who gives him some information about the life-forms on Arrakis—including the planet's sandworms.

ANALYSIS

Within the first few pages, *Dune* buries us in an avalanche of names—people, places, things, and concepts. Many of these new terms are explained, but many are not. We are forced either to wait until they are explained or try to figure things out using context clues. Most editions of *Dune* contain a glossary in the back, but it is not exhaustive, and there was no glossary when *Dune* was published serially in Startling Stories magazine in the early 1960s. It is comforting to realize that once we finish the book, almost everything makes sense. A second reading of *Dune*, particularly after reading the appendices, is often as enjoyable as the first, since we are then more aware of the implications of each event, small and large.

The novel immediately introduces us to Paul Atreides, who is the novel's main character. Although Paul is fifteen years old when the story begins, he never seems to act like a child or even a teenager. When the reverend mother tests him, he shows some mild arrogance and petulance, but no more than any adult undergoing such a test would. Paul's success with the test and his resistance to a great amount of pain make him seem even older. One idea that is not fully explored in *Dune* is the reverend mother's suggestion that Paul may be an animal instead of a human being. Prior to the test, Paul recites to himself a kind of mantra that partially explains the differences between animals and human beings: "Animal pleasures remain close to sensation levels and avoid the perceptual . . . the human requires a background grid through which to see the universe." These semiscientific, semireligious phrases are puzzling, and since they are never really explained, it is difficult to understand the difference between the author's definitions of animal and human. Judging from the test, however, it seems that people like the reverend mother believe that some human beings act just like animals and react to everything by instinct. What separates animals from humans, she believes, is the ability for humans to close off pain mentally and to use the rational mind to overcome instinctual and irrational impulses. The mantra that Paul recites seems to help him withstand the pain of the reverend mother's test.

The first few pages of *Dune* foreshadow that something destructive is in store for Duke Leto and the Atreides family. For example, the reverend mother warns that something terrible is going to happen to the Atreides family and that Paul's father, the duke, will die soon. When she suggests that Paul could be the Kwisatz Haderach, we begin to think this may be an important role in the preservation of the Atreides family. The reverend mother's warnings concern Paul, who thinks she speaks "as though [his] father were dead." Furthermore, Paul's dream about the caves and the girl who calls him Usul also seems to be a premonition of Paul's future and the novel's future events.

Although Paul is *Dune*'s main character, Herbert shifts perspective freely from character to character within a single page or even within a few paragraphs. We read the reverend mother's thoughts one moment, and Jessica's thoughts the next moment. Herbert's narrative technique provides us with an extraordinary amount of information, which is enriching, but also confusing. His narrative is flooded with countless names and concepts.

The technique becomes more familiar as the novel progresses. Eventually, Herbert allows us to know what each character thinks and feels consistently. Herbert's tactic provides as much information as possible about the characters and their world, but it removes much of the dramatic tension that might exist if we were less aware of the characters' intentions and motivations.

BOOK I (CONTINUED)

From Paul's meeting with the duke to Paul's concern over Mohiam's warnings

SUMMARY

We learn from the introductory biographical note, as well as from Dr. Yueh's own thoughts, that he is the traitor to the Atreides. Paul is joined by his father, Duke Leto, in the training room. Leto admits that they are walking into a trap set by Baron Harkonnen, but he believes that the Atreides can survive if they keep their eyes open. Leto reveals to Paul that the Harkonnens have been stockpiling melange, the spice drug, and plan to destroy the production of it on Arrakis while also obliterating the Atreides. Destruction of the spice supply would drive the prices of melange so high that the Harkonnens would gain control, while the Atreides shoulder the blame for the high prices. Leto tries to allay Paul's fears; Leto believes that the Atreides can beat the sneaky baron at his own game.

Soon the Atreides arrive on planet Arrakis. Lady Jessica meets her new servant, Shadout Mapes, who is a Fremen—a native of Arrakis. The native has been sent to test Jessica, and since she is a Bene Gesserit, a member of a special ancient school for women, Jessica passes the test. Jessica correctly identifies a strange knife that Mapes shows her, calling it a maker. Mapes refers to Jessica as "the One."

Jessica then goes to find Paul but instead finds Dr. Yueh. Paul is sleeping in the next room. Jessica and Yueh discuss Arrakeen politics, particularly the fact that some natives resent their rulers for the extravagant use of water on a planet that has practically no water. Other natives believe that the Atreides bring hope to Arrakis, in contrast to the previous Harkonnen rule. Yueh, who is desperately trying to conceal his traitorous plans from Jessica, who has Bene Gesserit mind abilities, reveals one small truth: his wife, also a Bene Gesserit, was taken and presumably killed by the Harkonnens.

In Paul's bedroom, a small robotic probe appears from behind the headboard and tries to kill him, but Paul manages to escape. The Atreides troops find a man beneath the palace, where he had been controlling the deadly robotic probe. Meanwhile, Jessica discovers the palace greenhouse, where thousands of plants are given hundreds of gallons of water per day. She also discovers a note from another Bene Gesserit, Lady Fenring, who belatedly warns Jessica about the assassination attempt on Paul. Fenring warns that a traitor is in their midst. Paul runs into the greenhouse, and Jessica tells him of the message.

The duke, rattled by the attempt on his son's life, attempts to move on with business, assigning Halleck, the war master, to convince the spice miners of Arrakis to continue working for the Atreides.

The duke meets with Paul and Thufir Hawat, the master of assassins. Hawat tries to resign for his failure to protect Paul, but the duke refuses to let him. The duke calls a meeting of all his men. They make several plans: to infiltrate the spice smugglers' network and win their support; to prepare for the impending Harkonnen trap; to raid in secret the Harkonnen spice reserves on another planet; and to recruit the Fremen as warriors to fight any possible threat. The Atreides also discuss Liet, the mysterious, perhaps godlike leader of the Fremen. While at the meeting, Duncan Idaho returns, along with a Fremen leader, Stilgar. Duncan, the swordmaster, has won Stilgar's respect, and the duke, with his respectful attitude, also wins Stilgar's respect. Stilgar offers Duncan a place in his sietch, a protective cave, and with the duke's blessing, Duncan agrees to join the Fremen. As the meeting breaks up, Paul recalls the Reverend Mother Mohiam's warning that his father would not be alive for long on Arrakis.

SUMMARY & ANALYSIS

ANALYSIS

This section of *Dune* introduces us to Arrakis, the desert world that is the setting for most of the novel. The most important aspect of life on Arrakis is the need for water, and there are signs of this need everywhere. There is the greenhouse, which uses thousands of gallons of water a day to water its plants. The greenhouse is a show of extravagance but also a sign of hope that the landscape of Arrakis can be transformed into a lush paradise. A small cut that Jessica makes on Shadout Mapes stops bleeding almost immediately; such swift clotting is necessary when water is so precious. To show his respect for the duke, Stilgar spits on the table. Stilgar gives up some of his moisture, which is a precious gift. Later in the book there are more examples of the supreme importance of water for the Fremen. Fremen do not use the word blood when referring to an important, limited life force, but instead they use water.

The lack of water is a sign of the planet's precarious ecology. One of *Dune's* themes is mankind's ability to live within a planet's ecological system and humanity's ability to disrupt that system, with either good or ill results. Frank Herbert got his initial idea for *Dune* after studying a governmental ecological project designed to halt the spread of sand dunes on the Oregon coastline. Examples of humanity altering a natural, ecological process can be found throughout *Dune*, but the most apparent is the Fremen's hopes to change Arrakis from a desert planet to a lush, Edenic paradise. Such a transformation sounds ideal. However, even changes made with good intentions can have negative consequences. Herbert is well aware of the ambiguity in ecological preservation—*Dune* stops short of taking a definitive stance on how humans should interact with their environment.

Another important development in this section is the Fremen's identification of Jessica as being a Bene Gesserit. We learn that the Bene Gesserit have, some time in the distant past, traveled the galaxy to many worlds, implanting generic myths about themselves that later generations of Bene Gesserit could use to their advantage if they become stranded on an unfamiliar planet. In this case, the Fremen have learned legends of a Bene Gesserit woman who will be the mother of their savior. The legends were originally intended to allow a Bene Gesserit to find help if she needs it and to be accepted by the general population if she found herself on a new planet. In the case of Jessica and the planet Arrakis, as hinted by the quotes from Princess Irulan before each section, the legends will be more accurate than ever before.

The sheer size and complexity of the world Herbert creates is overwhelming. Aside from the number of main characters, the action is set against a large background of intergalactic politics. At the core of the story is the idea that a simple desert planet like Arrakis can play a major role in determining the course of the galactic empire. The importance of Arrakis, however, lies not so much in Paul, but in the planet's production of melange, the spice drug to which so many people are addicted. The incredible value of the spice drug is the reason the Atreides are so suspicious that the emperor is handing Arrakis over to them. All of the characters, from Duke Leto to Paul to Jessica, know that the Atreides are walking into a trap. While the duke may hope that he can avoid the trap, Jessica and Paul know the truth: the duke will not live much longer. Throughout the novel, there is a tension between fate and Paul's struggle to guide his own future.

BOOK I (CONTINUED)

From Hawat's interception of the baron's note to Kynes's discussion of Arrakis's ecology

SUMMARY

Baron Harkonnen's plans are coming to fruition: Thufir Hawat, the master of assassins, intercepts a note, allegedly from the baron to Lady Jessica, that implicates her in a plot to betray Duke Leto. The duke does not believe the allegation, but he recognizes it as a Harkonnen plot, and he decides that in order to trap the Harkonnens, he must pretend to fall into the trap. He decides to allow Hawat and Duncan Idaho, his swordmaster, to think that Jessica may be guilty, though he does not actually believe the allegations.

Some of the Fremen have started calling Paul the Mahdi, or "the one who will lead us to paradise." This follows the prophecy that their messianic savior will arrive as the child of a Bene Gesserit, like Jessica.

The duke tells Paul about the Harkonnen plot to turn the duke against Lady Jessica but warns him to tell no one else. The duke has plans to use his "propaganda corps" to secure the loyalty of the people of Arrakis, but he warns Paul that if anything goes wrong Paul should make use of his Mahdi status to gain the Fremen's respect.

The duke and Paul then meet Dr. Kynes, the Arrakis ecologist. Kynes has been ordered to betray the Atreides, but he finds himself impressed by them despite his low expectations of their character. Kynes explains the use of stillsuits, special outfits that contain the amount of moisture the body uses up and which are able to recycle the majority of the body's moisture. As Kynes interacts more and more with Paul, he finds that Paul oddly seems to fit the legends of the Mahdi. Kynes is also surprised to find that Leto is a penetrating man who seems interested in Kynes's plans to make Arrakis an Edenic paradise.

Kynes takes the duke and Paul to visit a spice-mining operation. While they are there, the roaming spice factory is attacked by a giant sandworm. The duke takes control and makes sure to save all the miners, leaving the spice behind. The duke's concern for human life over spice impresses Kynes. As the duke leaves and his ship flies away, Paul spots two men that he correctly identifies as Fremen, though Kynes tries to hide that fact. Paul's mysterious skills and the duke's concern for his workers' lives impress Kynes even more.

The duke holds a dinner party for the distinguished members of Arrakeen society, the wealthy members of the planet. Kynes attends, and he is surprised when Jessica expresses her hope that one day Arrakis will be a lush paradise. Kynes asks her if she brings "the shortening of the way," which translates to Kwisatz Haderach. Jessica does not have the chance to answer, but it is clear that Kynes is becoming more intrigued by Jessica and Paul.

At the dinner party, Jessica realizes that there is at least one spy present, a Guild banker. Paul seems to have recognized the banker's behavior as well and banters with him. Jessica notes that the banker seems to be terrified of Kynes. The duke engages Kynes in discussing the possibility of changing Arrakis's climate, and Kynes reluctantly admits that there may be enough water on Arrakis to start the process of making it an Eden.

ANALYSIS

The third section introduces a complex set of character interactions. The plot becomes increasingly dense and almost incomprehensible. At the center of the plot is a new character, Dr. Kynes. We already know that Dr. Kynes, the ecologist, or, as he calls himself, planetologist, has been ordered to sabotage the Atreides's efforts at making any money off Arrakis. However, Kynes's initial agreement to sabotage the Atreides was more due to his own desire to hurt the Atreides's plan, rather than due to the Harkonnens' bribing or bullying. Thus, Kynes is surprised when the Atreides quickly earn his respect. Kynes is impressed by Duke Leto's honest concern for the lives of men that he has not even met, and Paul fascinates him because he fulfills many of the Fremen prophecies. Paul's role as a Mahdi for the Fremen is important to Kynes since Kynes is Liet, a godlike figure for the Fremen. Kynes's fascination with Paul becomes more important later in the novel. For now, Kynes is still watching and weighing his options.

The dinner scene in this section is one of the funniest and most macabre scenes in the book. The dinner party is an uncomfortable affair, with many people using one another to further their own goals. Duke Leto uses the dinner as an opportunity to analyze the elite members of the new Arrakis world, but he also embarrasses himself by making it clear how much he intends to change their lifestyle by changing the planet's ecology. Leto is also tortured because he must pretend that he distrusts his wife. Kynes has an alliance with Tuek, a head smuggler on Arrakis, and can intimidate the Guild banker-spy. Jessica recognizes that the banker is a Harkonnen spy, and there is a tense scene in which Paul nearly gets in a fight with him. Paul and Jessica are also aware that Kynes tells several lies in the course of the dinner. As for the rest of the dinner party attendees, they are interested in finding out how they can take advantage of their new rulers. Herbert fills the party scene with tension and humor while revealing a wealth of information about the characters.

The placement of the dinner-party scene within the scope of the novel is important. The dinner party represents the high point of the duke's brief reign on Arrakis. From here on, problems will mount as the Harkonnen trap unfolds and unravels the duke's power. Throughout the dinner celebration, there is a sense that the duke's reign is fated to end, which the reverend mother emphasized earlier in the novel. Thus far, Herbert imbues the tone of *Dune* with a sense of fatalism—and the feeling that once certain events are put into motion, they will progress to a particular unavoidable conclusion. For instance, Jessica and the reverend mother knew that once the emperor gave Arrakis to the duke, the duke's situation was hopeless—he would fail and most likely die. Paul is already beginning to develop a premonition of doom, and he struggles with this "sense of terrible purpose" throughout the novel.

BOOK I (CONTINUED)

From Duncan's drunk visit to the end of Book I

SUMMARY

A drunk Duncan Idaho, the swordmaster, stumbles into the Atreides castle. Jessica chastises Duncan, who in his drunken state reveals that he suspects that Jessica is a spy for the Harkonnens. Jessica, shocked, calls Hawat to meet with Duncan. She confronts him with his suspicions and tries to convince Hawat that their beliefs are irrational. Jessica explains that it is more logical to believe that the

Harkonnens are making Hawat suspicious of her. But Hawat is loyal only to Duke Leto, and he cannot eliminate his suspicion of Jessica. Jessica uses the "Voice" on him, a semi-magical tone of voice that forces Hawat to obey whatever she says. The Voice surprises and disturbs Hawat and makes him think that Jessica is an even more dangerous enemy. When Jessica and Hawat part that night, he is still suspicious.

Late that night, Duke Leto is pondering a strange note he received. He hears an odd sound and investigates, discovering the dead bodies of Tuek and Shadout Mapes. Yueh has shut off the house generators and the shield, leaving the Atreides castle vulnerable to attack. Yueh attacks Leto and informs him that he is placing a false tooth in the duke's mouth. The tooth will release a great poisonous gas when the duke closes his mouth tightly. He feels badly that he has betrayed the duke, so he tells Duke Leto to bite down on the tooth when he is brought before Baron Harkonnen. This way, Yueh can kill the baron and avenge his wife's death. However, Yueh still feels some guilt for killing the duke, so he has arranged for Paul and Jessica to escape safely. He takes Leto's ducal ring to give to Paul as sign of his true intentions for Jessica and Paul to be spared.

Sometime shortly thereafter, Jessica and Paul are kidnapped by the Harkonnens. The Harkonnen guards fly them into the desert, presumably to kill the pair. Jessica seduces the two guards and they fight over her until one guard kills the other. Jessica then distracts the remaining guard long enough for Paul to kill him. Paul and Jessica discover a small bundle inside the ship containing food, stillsuits, and other provisions, as well as the ducal ring. As they free themselves, more ornithopters, or small flying ships, appear over the horizon, heading toward them.

Yueh confronts Baron Harkonnen and demands to know what has happened to his wife. As Yueh expected, the baron has killed her, and the baron then orders Piter to kill Yueh as well. The baron's men bring Duke Leto before the baron, who gloats over his success at defeating the duke. He demands to know where Jessica and Paul have fled, but the duke does not know. The baron threatens to torture Leto. Leto bites down on the poison false tooth, emitting a gas that kills Piter and all the guards, but the baron escapes. One of the Sardaukar, the elite troops of the emperor, demands to see the duke's body, as the emperor had requested. The emperor's request causes the baron to lose face in front of his men.

Paul and Jessica are now hiding in a tent from the ornithopters. Fortunately, Duncan Idaho is piloting the ornithopter on instructions from Yueh. Yueh had helped Duncan escape from the baron's men. Duncan hides Paul and Jessica and then leaves to help the other surviving Atreides men. During this time, Paul changes: his intelligence has become very cold and calculating, but it has also become very powerful. He is able to think ahead of his mother, a Bene Gesserit. Paul reveals to Jessica that the duke always knew she was innocent of treachery. She grieves, but he finds he is unable to grieve with her. As Paul sits, he suddenly has a vision: his intelligence increases, and he has become hyperaware because of the spice he has been eating in his food. He suddenly has a prophetic dream and sees thousands of possible futures. Paul can have these prophesies because of the sudden increased power of his mind and his Mentat-style training. He tells Jessica that she will give birth to a daughter, despite the fact that Jessica has not told anyone she is pregnant. Paul also reveals that both he and Jessica are Harkonnens—the baron was Jessica's unknown father.

ANALYSIS

This section describes the key strategies of the Harkonnen trap, showing the baron's military intelligence. The trap's complexity suggests that the baron has spent many years devising his plot against the Atreides. The Harkonnen trap includes many different features. First, to bypass the Atreides energy-based defense shields—intended to block lasguns, or laser guns—the Harkonnens use projectile weaponry like bullets, missiles, and artillery fire. Second, the emperor is a party to the baron's treachery. Therefore, the Sardaukar, the emperor's ruthless elite troops, will help the baron destroy the Atreides's troops. The Houses of the Landsraad, the overarching group of families that controls most of the galaxy, would be very upset if they discovered that the emperor had supported the defeat of the Atreides and would likely band together to oust him. To prevent the Landsraad from finding out, the Sardaukar disguise themselves as Harkonnen soldiers. Finally, the baron intends to install one of his own brethren—Rabban, one of his lesser nephews—to rule Arrakis after the Harkonnens take over. The baron wants Rabban to oppress the Arrakeen people and make them hate him, so that when the baron's beloved nephew Feyd-Rautha arrives to take Rabban's place, he will be welcomed as a hero.

The baron does not just fight against the Atreides, but he also defies his own family members, as well as the Houses of Landsraad, the governing board to which he belongs. His outright abuse of his relationships suggests that he will not be in power for much longer.

Paul, on the other hand, must learn to handle his new superpowers so that he does not abuse them. After the death of Paul's father, Paul's character transforms physically, mentally, and emotionally. He kills his first man: the guard on the ornithopter. As he hides in the tent, he also becomes aware of the "terrible purpose" in life that will haunt him for the rest of the novel. Paul must remember his training as a Mentat but also as a Bene Gesserit. Mentats are trained to think only in logical, rational terms; their primary skill is calculating any and every bit of information. Their minds record and analyze everything they see. However, Paul's mother has also trained him in the more intuitive, spiritual, and mystical powers of the Bene Gesserit. Paul's success lies in balancing his powers of logic and intuition.

Paul's ability to handle his new powers is made even more difficult by his use of the magical melange, the spice drug. Melange heightens the user's awareness of the senses, both rational and spiritual. Paul's human brain uses only a portion of its potential until he eats the melange spice. He becomes hyperaware of everything around him, and his two schools of training combine to allow him to notice every detail around him, and then plug into a vast mental calculator that computes all the possible outcomes of the future. Some of this computation is mystical as well; there is no logical way that Paul could know his sister would be known as St. Alia of the Knife or that he would meet a girl who would call him Usul. Paul has become a kind of superhuman, capable of combining the skills of a Mentat and a Bene Gesserit. The Fremen will respect Paul's ability to balance his powers, suggesting that unlike the baron, Paul will rise to become the leader of the universe and will become the Mahdi.

BOOK II

From the beginning of Book II to Rabban's arrival as the ruler of Arrakis

SUMMARY

> *"This is the bond of water. We know the rites. A man's flesh is his own; the water belongs to the tribe."*
> (See QUOTATIONS, p. 53)

Paul is still in the tent, revealing the vast extent of his newfound powers to his mother, Jessica. She thinks Paul is the Kwisatz Haderach, a person with the power to change the universe, but he tells her to forget that idea—he is "something unexpected." Using his heightened awareness of the future's possibilities, Paul realizes that he is a product of the Bene Gesserit's efforts to reinvigorate the human gene pool, but the form that the rejuvenation will take is that of a jihad, or a holy war. The war, led by the remaining Atreides troops and the Fremen, will spread across the universe and disperse the beliefs and laws of the conquerors. The idea of the jihad frightens Paul, and he resolves to try to stop it, if he can.

Paul and Jessica continue to wait for Duncan Idaho's return. When he does not arrive by nightfall, they decide to move to a new hiding place. As they leave, they see Harkonnen ornithopters blasting the surrounding area, looking for them.

Meanwhile, Thufir Hawat, the Atreides master of assassins, confers with a Fremen elsewhere on the planet. Hawat is amazed that ten legions of Sardaukar and Harkonnen troops were used in the attack—the venture would cost fifty years' worth of the entire yearly income of Arrakis. The Fremen press Hawat to allow them to take away the bodies of the dead Atreides troops in order to reuse their water. Hawat reluctantly agrees and this secures a sort of bond between the two groups. Hawat is then impressed when several Fremen overpower an ornithopter piloted by Sardaukar and crash it into an enemy troop carrier—it is a feat of combat skill and daring unlike any he has seen. Just as Hawat and the Fremen prepare to move out of the area, the Harkonnen attack and capture Hawat.

Paul and Jessica discover, to their relief, that Duncan and Kynes are piloting the ornithopters surrounding them. Kynes takes them to an ecological testing facility, where they discover that Kynes is also Liet, the godlike, supreme leader of the Fremen. Paul and Kynes negotiate: Paul plans to use the Fremen and their skills to blackmail the emperor into putting Paul and the Atreides on the throne of Arrakis. If the emperor refuses, Paul will show evidence to the Houses of the Landsraad that the emperor sent Sardaukar to destroy the Atreides. If the Landsraad knew that the emperor helped to attack the Atreides, the houses of the universe would unite against the emperor in an immense intergalactic war. Kynes is skeptical, but when Paul pledges his allegiance to Kynes, even at the expense of his own life, Kynes is instantly loyal to Paul in return.

The Sardaukar attack Kynes's facility, and Kynes helps Jessica and Paul escape; Duncan is killed in the battle. Paul and Jessica take an ornithopter and flee their Harkonnen pursuers. They fly into a sandstorm to cover their tracks, barely keeping the flying machine above the dangerous winds.

The baron's guard captain tells him that Jessica and Paul must be dead, as no one can stay alive in such a storm. The baron, however, is angry that the captain did not see the dead bodies. The captain also reports that he believes Kynes is a traitor, and the baron orders him to be killed in what looks like an accidental death. The captain also informs the baron that Thufir Hawat has been captured, and the baron decides to convince Hawat to become his personal Mentat. The baron's nephew Rabban arrives to take control of Arrakis. The baron orders Rabban to squeeze the populace of Arrakis, and to oppress them into submission.

ANALYSIS

> *They were all caught up in the need of their race to renew its scattered inheritance, to cross and mingle and infuse their bloodlines in a great new pooling of genes. And the race knew only one sure way for this—the ancient way . . . jihad.*

(See QUOTATIONS, p. 52)

One of the most important motifs in *Dune* is Paul's concern that he will be the instigator of a jihad, or holy war, led by the Fremen under his banner. Paul worries that the jihad will spread across the universe as the Fremen and the House of Atreides kill everyone in their path. The reason for this jihad, Paul believes, is that it will reinvigorate the human gene pool, which has been stagnant during the last 10,000 years. Paul wants to resist these possible futures, and he will spend the rest of the novel analyzing his options in every situation, trying to predict their outcome and attempting to take the course that will prevent such a long and bloody war. The jihad is the embodiment of Paul's sense of "terrible purpose," a cursed fate that he feels he must resist.

Another important motif in this section is water. On Arrakis, water is much more important than blood because blood cannot exist without water. For example, instead of mourning the loss of lives, Fremen quickly treat the Atreides corpses so they can extract their water; the Fremen ask for the "water bond" with Hawat, which is the equivalent of a blood oath. Now in a situation in which water is a scarce resource, Jessica finds herself thinking more in terms of conserving water. Spitting and crying are considered noble acts because they involve a sacrifice of precious water.

The meeting between Paul and Kynes is a key plot development. Paul wins the loyalty of the Fremen's secular and religious leader by offering his own unmitigated loyalty. As a result, he recognizes the importance of the Fremen to "desert power," which is required to maintain control of the planet Arrakis. However, Paul is earnest in his offer of help and in his desire to make Arrakis into an Eden full of plants and animals. Paul's alliance with the Fremen is partially made out of political necessity—without the Fremen's help, the Atreides are lost—but also because he believes in and supports the Fremen's desire to change their world for the better. The meeting scene is also important because it sets up Paul to replace the godlike Kynes as the spiritual and military leader of the Fremen, following the Harkonnens' murder of Kynes.

BOOK II (CONTINUED)

From Paul and Jessica's ride through the sandstorm to Paul's meeting with Chani

SUMMARY

> "We must depend not so much on the bravery of individuals, you see, as upon the bravery of a whole population."

(See QUOTATIONS, p. 51)

After four hours of riding through the sandstorm, Paul and Jessica finally fly out and discover that Harkonnen ornithopters are no longer pursuing them. Paul lands their ornithopter near a large rocky area, and as they run toward the rocks, a sandworm appears and eats the ship.

Paul and Jessica trudge through the desert. They must rest by day and move by night to avoid heat exhaustion. They reach the end of the rocky zone and must cross open desert to reach the next one. While they are making their way down a slope, Jessica gets caught in a sandslide, and Paul abandons the pack to the sand to save her. He rescues his mother and, with great effort, recovers the pack.

Meanwhile, Gurney Halleck, the Atreides war master, has survived the Harkonnen attack, and he meets with Staban Tuek, the son of the now-deceased Esmar Tuek. Halleck decides to join the smuggler's operation, hoping to one day use it to his advantage against the Harkonnens.

Paul and Jessica plant a thumper, a device that makes a rhythmic thumping noise, to distract the sandworm while they shuffle across the desert to the next rock zone—they must walk without rhythm so they do not attract the worm. They reach the rock zone, but are followed by the worm, which reaches over the rock's facade and nearly catches them. Luckily, another thumper, in the distance, draws the worm away. At the top of the rock zone, Fremen accost and threaten them.

Elsewhere, Kynes stumbles alone through the desert without a stillsuit. The Harkonnens had left him to die. As he tries to walk, delirious from the heat, he imagines that his dead father—the planetologist for Arrakis before Kynes—is speaking to him. His father chides him for helping Paul and lectures his son on trying to educate the Fremen about their planet to help create great ecological changes on Arrakis. Kynes's father also warns that a "pre-spice mass" is developing underground, which will soon explode and kill Kynes. A pre-spice mass is a stage in the growth of melange in which the spice explodes in order to get to the sun and air above ground and complete the melange cycle. The father continues his harangue, reciting the plans he made decades ago to change Arrakis, changes that Kynes had initiated during his lifetime. Finally, the pre-spice mass explodes, killing Kynes.

Back at the rock zone, the Fremen interrogate Paul. The wise leader of the Fremen introduces himself as Stilgar, who Paul has seen before. Keynes had ordered Stilgar to find Paul, but he is skeptical about taking Jessica as well. Jessica then pulls a knife on

Stilgar and holds it to his throat, while Paul runs and hides in the shadows. Stilgar is impressed that Jessica is knowledgeable of the "weirding way," a form of combat. Jessica notices the Fremen's use of a language called Chakobsa and makes an assumption about their culture, guessing correctly that they will recognize the term gom jabbar. Stilgar makes a deal with her: if she will teach the Fremen this combat style, then Paul and Jessica can live with the Fremen. One of the Fremen is Chani, Kynes's daughter, whom Paul has seen before in a dream.

ANALYSIS

Paul is destined to fill one of the most common roles in fantasy and science fiction: that of "the One," the savior who will lead his adopted people to victory over their enemies. In the earth's history, messianic figures are usually very passive: Buddha, Jesus, and Muhammad were all fairly peaceful people, though much violence has occurred in the name of Jesus or Muhammad since their deaths. But in fantasy and science fiction, "the One" often leads his people to victory by using violence. Paul is acutely aware of the significance of his power and the bloody jihad that may be an unavoidable consequence of that power.

The interaction between the Fremen and the Atreides in this scene is complex. The characters often make references to a back history that has not been mentioned earlier and, sometimes, is never explained. For instance, Jessica manages to attack and subdue Stilgar, the leader of the Fremen. Jessica's feat is impressive, since we have seen how easily the Fremen butcher the Sardaukar. We assume that Jessica's supernatural abilities are based on her Bene Gesserit training, but this is unclear. After Jessica's training is called the "weirding way" and we hear more about the Missionaria Protectiva, the Bene Gesserit mission to spread legends in the universe, we become even more confused.

Like the worlds in other major works of science fiction or fantasy, such as J. R. R. Tolkien's *The Lord of the Rings*, Herbert's fictional world is rich in detail and back history, but that information is often only hinted at in the course of the novel. Tolkien integrates these hints within his story, and they do not distract us because the history of his made-up planet is similar enough to real human legends and folklore. *Dune*, however, is set against 10,000 years of human political history, including the development of a set of human beings with almost mystical abilities, known as the Bene Gesserit. Thus, it is common to feel disoriented while reading *Dune*. This does not mean that there are aspects of *Dune* that are impossible to understand. However, the novel requires focused attention to details and context clues.

Religion plays an important role in *Dune* because it helps establish and maintain traditions, even though the traditions themselves are fabricated.

A key tactical facet of the Bene Gesserit is the Missionaria Protectiva, which has planted "safety valves" throughout Arrakis. These safety valves are stories spread by a Bene Gesserit who went to Arrakis a long time ago. The stories included a tale about a savior who would lead the people of Arrakis to paradise. If a Bene Gesserit came to Arrakis many years later, she would be safe from harm. She would reference the old stories, and the Arrakis people would believe she was their savior. The Arrakis people believe that Jessica and Paul are their saviors and that they will help Arrakis become a lush, green paradise. The Bene Gesserit use these fabricated traditions to preserve and protect their people. Although their religious beliefs are made up, the traditions serve an important purpose in spreading the knowledge and power of the Bene Gesserit to other worlds.

BOOK II (CONTINUED)

From Stilgar leading Jessica and Paul to the Fremen stronghold to Lady Fenring's plans to seduce Feyd-Rautha

SUMMARY

Stilgar and the rest of the Fremen lead Paul and Jessica to a Fremen stronghold. Although Jessica has successfully competed against him, Stilgar advises her not to challenge his authority, because the Fremen would not trust her as a leader, as she is "not of the sand." Stilgar reveals that the Fremen have been preparing a load of spice to use to bribe the Guild, which has a monopoly on space travel and banking. The Fremen hope that in return, the Guild will not allow the Harkonnens to establish spy satellites that could monitor the Fremen. Stilgar tells Jessica that the Fremen hope to transform Arrakis into a lush, Edenic paradise. He knows it will not happen for many generations but that it will happen in the future. To her surprise, Jessica also discovers that the Fremen travel by riding on the back of sandworms.

Stilgar realizes he must secure a place for Jessica in the Fremen society. He notes that their own reverend mother is old and may need a replacement. The idea of becoming a reverend mother shocks Jessica. Stilgar mentions the legendary prophecy that the son of a Bene Gesserit holds the key to their future, and Jessica knows she must give some sort of sign to prove she can fulfill the prophecy. She suddenly has an intuitive vision, and in a trance she recites several biblical lines that excite the Fremen. Stilgar accepts Jessica as a possible future reverend mother. Jessica does not reveal to him that she is carrying a child. Paul has prophesied that the child will be a girl and will be known as St. Alia.

Jamis, the Fremen who Paul battled on the rock zone, challenges Paul to a duel to the death. Paul reluctantly agrees; he does not want to kill anyone. Paul has a difficult time fighting Jamis in knife-to-knife combat because he is used to fighting with body energy shields. Finally, Paul kills Jamis, and the Fremen are impressed. They take Jamis away to use the water in his corpse. Stilgar gives Paul a secret Sietch Tabr name called Usul, which means the base of a pillar. Paul then chooses a name for himself, Muad'Dib, which anyone can refer to him as. Muad'Dib is the name of a mouse on Arrakis, an animal that is considered wise by the Fremen.

At Jamis's funeral, the Fremen offer his water to Paul, and the water is later deposited in a special basin under the caverns. Afterward, Chani, Kynes's daughter, asks Paul to play a song on Jamis's baliset, a guitarlike instrument. He plays a love song, which disturbs Jessica; she does not want Paul consorting with a low-born Fremen woman. Paul suddenly recognizes that his mother will be responsible for causing the jihad.

Meanwhile, on the home world of the Harkonnens, Baron Harkonnen's nephew Feyd-Rautha is set to fight in a gladiatorial ring. Visiting the baron are Count Fenring and Lady Fenring. Feyd-Rautha is smitten by Lady Fenring's beauty. Feyd-Rautha has set up a scheme to make the gladiatorial challenge seem more dangerous than it is; his challenger will not be drugged, as usual, but will have a secret word, implanted hypnotically, that will make him immobile. The scheme has been arranged by the baron's new Mentat, Thufir Hawat. Feyd-Rautha's opponent in the gladiatorial ring, he discovers, is one of the former Atreides soldiers. Feyd-Rautha uses the secret word and kills the soldier, though for a moment he feels threatened. Feyd-Rautha glories in his win, while Count and Lady Fenring discuss plans for Lady Fenring to seduce Feyd-Rautha and become pregnant with his child in order to continue the Bene Gesserit genetic program.

ANALYSIS

In this section, the Fremen officially welcome Paul into their clan, and he starts to fill the role of savior of the Fremen. Unfortunately, for Paul's acceptance to be complete, he must kill Jamis. The ritualistic shedding of blood is a powerful step in Paul's development: regardless of his newfound hyperintelligence, he is still only sixteen years old. Paul's win also serves to induct him into many of the tribe's rituals. He accepts the water that was once part of Jamis, a Fremen, and he, in turn, becomes a Fremen himself. Paul learns about the great water well, one of thousands, which will eventually be used to turn Arrakis into a Garden of Eden. The Fremen plan to save up enough water until they are able to start a complex ecological plan to change Arrakis's climate. Also interesting is that Paul becomes part of the Fremen clan not because of his supernatural powers, logical ability, or technological know-how. Instead, Paul earns his membership in the clan when he kills another man during an almost prehistoric show of power: the duel.

Paul's killing of Jamis is an important rite of passage. Jessica makes sure that Paul realizes the gravity of what he has done: she reminds him that he should not take pleasure in his "triumph." For Paul, the victory is bittersweet, and he mourns the loss of Jamis, while understanding that Jamis's death was necessary to save more lives in the end. Other rites of passage are taking place as well, as there are hints in this section of a future relationship between Chani and Paul when Paul serenades her. Paul's connection with Chani will serve his messianic purposes—bonding with the daughter of Liet, Kynes, can only help his development as a religious leader among the Fremen.

Also in this section is a growing tension between Paul and his mother, which foreshadows the tension that would be caused by a jihad. Jessica is a Bene Gesserit. At times, she has resisted the orders and training of the Bene Gesserit, most significantly by having a boy rather than a girl, but they have always influenced her decisions. Jessica accepts her role as the mother of the savior, according to the implanted legends of the Missionaria Protectiva; thus she is strengthening her ties to the Bene Gesserit. As a result, Jessica becomes increasingly concerned about Paul and his future role in both the Fremen society and the universe as a whole. She realizes he is the Kwisatz Haderach, according to the legend of the Missionaria Protectiva, and the Bene Gesserit have very specific plans for Paul to alter the gene pool of the universe. Paul, however, knows that there can be only one result of the Bene Gesserit's plans—war.

BOOK II (CONTINUED)

From Paul and Jessica going to Sietch Tabr through Chani leading Paul away to make love

SUMMARY

> *The drug had him again and he thought: So many times you've given me comfort and forgetfulness.*
> (See QUOTATIONS, p. 55)

The Fremen lead Paul and Jessica to Sietch Tabr, the home of Stilgar and his particular troop of Fremen. There, Paul and Jessica discover that Kynes, who is the Liet to the Fremen and Chani's father, is dead. At the sietch, Paul meets Harah, Jamis's wife, who is now bound to marry or serve Paul. Her sons are also entrusted to Paul's care. Paul accepts Harah as a servant, though not as a wife. Harah takes him through the sietch, which the tribe will soon have to abandon now that the Sardaukar are hunting them. Life goes on as usual in the sietch: even as they prepare to leave, children are taking classes and workers are preparing programs, including a plan for a system of dew collectors, to run in their absence.

The Fremen hold a ceremony, welcoming Jessica into the clan as their reverend mother and replacing their old one, who will soon die. As part of the ceremony, Jessica is required to drink a strange liquid from a sack. Using her Bene Gesserit powers, Jessica turns her mind inward and chemically transforms the poison into a safe liquid. The liquid in the sack touches her mouth, and a chemical reaction spreads through the sack, making the liquid safe for Jessica to drink.

While the ceremony continues, Jessica feels trapped within herself. The dying reverend mother comes before Jessica, embraces her. The reverend mother then allows her spirit to be absorbed into Jessica's body and mind. With the mother's spirit comes the entire history of the Bene Gesserit and humanity itself, back thousands of years, even before the rise of the Bene Gesserit. At the same time, the unborn child inside Jessica is flooded with the same memories and awareness, and only Jessica's love prevents the child from going insane.

Jessica tells the Fremen to drink the water from the sack so that they may enjoy the heightened awareness that will come from the melangelike liquid. Chani leads Paul away, and they presumably make love.

ANALYSIS

The spice drug's effect on both Jessica and Paul raises their awareness to unnatural dimensions. In the case of Jessica, the drug allows her to converse with and then absorb the spirit of the previous reverend mother. At the same time, Jessica incorporates the spirits of all reverend mothers before her and absorbs all their memories. The inclusion in the novel of drugs leading to mind-altering situations is not surprising, since Herbert wrote *Dune* in the 1960s, when drug experimentation was entering the mainstream consciousness of America. These drugs, however, seem to have beneficial effects—namely, they heighten intellectual as well as sensual awareness. Jessica is able to read the memories of thousands of years of Bene Gesserit and find some meaning in their history. The spice drug, in such a pure form, allows Paul to see the "gray turmoil" of his future more clearly than ever before. Melange's effects suggest the delicacy of Paul's balance between two sides. He sees the Harkonnens and the emperor and the Bene Gesserit on one side, and the Fremen on the other, with himself walking a careful line between them.

Melange also heightens the awareness of the unborn child inside Jessica, suggesting that Alia will also have to cope with superhuman powers. Both of Jessica's children, Alia and Paul, do not experience a normal childhood. Even in the womb, Alia is conscious of herself and her place in the history of the universe. She is never an innocent child, but instead she is born with the knowledge of all the sins, problems, and pains of the past. As a result of Alia's precocious behavior, others see her as unnatural or evil.

Herbert's description of Alia reminds us of the concept of original sin. God banished Adam and Eve from the paradise of Eden because they did not obey him and ate the fruit of knowledge. According to Christianity, people are born with this "original sin," the sin of Adam and Eve. Alia's birth embodies the original sin, as she is literally born with the knowledge and collective consciousness

of humanity. The name Alia is also significant in the Judeo-Christian tradition. To make an aliyah is to go up toward God. The birth of Alia is the fulfillment of Jessica's belief in the Bene Gesserit, a religion. Thus, Jessica goes before her religion and presents them with her Alia. Alia, with her supernatural knowledge of the universe, is almost godlike in her abilities. We will learn later that Alia plays an important role in helping the Fremen transform their planet into a paradise, an Edenic world.

Book III

From the beginning of Book III to Paul teaching the smugglers a lesson

Summary

Two years have passed since the events in Book II. Baron Harkonnen fumes as he rushes through his private quarters searching for his guard captain. A slave boy whom the baron had been enjoying attempts to kill the baron. The baron surmises that Feyd-Rautha is responsible for planning the assassination. He quickly surmises the identity of the moles within the baron's guard, and he orders them to be killed immediately. The baron confronts Feyd-Rautha and chides him for the foolish attempt on his life. He tells the teenager that one day, not too far in the future, he will step down and allow Feyd-Rautha to succeed him. The baron also tells Feyd-Rautha that he will assign Thufir Hawat to watch over him, and Feyd-Rautha realizes that Hawat has been playing Feyd-Rautha and the baron against each other. Feyd-Rautha decides to wait, for now, and see what his uncle's plans are regarding the emperor.

The baron meets with Hawat. Hawat has asked the baron to send a message to Rabban, the baron's nephew, on Arrakis, but he has not said why. Hawat reveals to the baron his suspicion that the Empire uses the penal colony of Salusa Secundus as a training ground for the Sardaukar. Hawat explains that he believes that the emperor ordered the destruction of the House of Atreides because Duke Leto's men had trained a small fighting force whose skills nearly match those of the Sardaukar. Hawat points out that Arrakis is as brutal a place for training as Salusa Secundus; the Fremen are an even better fighting force than the Sardaukar. The baron recalls that he once suggested to Count Fenring the possibility of using Arrakis as a prison planet. Hawat suggests that the baron abandon all aid to Rabban and force him to oppress the people even more, so as to make Arrakis into a new Salusa Secundus.

On Arrakis, Paul is preparing to ride a sandworm for the first time. In the last two years, the Fremen have recognized him as a religious prophet. Paul is both a religious and a political leader. He is surrounded by Fedaykin, an elite, highly trained guard. His mother, now the new reverend mother, has become concerned about his role with the Fremen. She has given birth to a daughter, Alia. Chani has also given birth to a child, the product of her unofficial union with Paul. Paul's son is named Leto, like Paul's father. The Fremen do not easily accept Alia; since she was still in the womb when her mother took the spice drug, she took in all the memories of the previous Bene Gesserit, so she was aware of herself and was very intelligent even before she was born. Now, barely two years old, she can speak in complete, lucid sentences like an adult and walk easily.

Paul leaves his tent and meets with Stilgar, who gives him a thumper to call the sandworm. Other Fremen give him hooks and poles to use to grab on to the worm's side. Paul activates the thumper, and soon a giant worm is making its way toward him.

Far in the south of planet Arrakis, Jessica rests in the safety of the sietch warrens. Harah and Alia enter her room. Harah is concerned because Alia has been making the Fremen mothers uneasy. She speaks and carries herself like an adult, and they think she is a witch or possessed by a demon. Harah feels compassion for the young child and says she will try to make the other woman understand.

A Fremen messenger arrives and tells Jessica about a problem: some of the young Fremen men plan to push Paul into challenging Stilgar for leadership of the tribe after Paul rides the sandworm.

Back in the north, Paul succeeds in riding the sandworm he called with his thumper. Stilgar suggests they stop and camp for the night. Both of them realize that the young men will want Paul to challenge Stilgar soon. As they discuss the issue, they spot a smuggler ornithopter flying overhead. Paul decides to teach the smugglers a lesson not to invade Fremen territory.

ANALYSIS

During the two years between Book II and Book III, Paul establishes himself as a prophet, a powerful religious leader, to the Fremen. His combat skills are now legendary; for example, he has trained a squad of "death commandos" called Fedaykin, the most loyal and deadly soldiers on Arrakis. Alia has also caught the attention of the Fremen. Due to her unique experience in the womb, she is practically a reverend mother, just like Jessica. She is certainly one of the more disturbing creations in science fiction: a two-year-old who talks and thinks like an adult. Jessica accepts the young Alia almost as an equal, allowing her to attend and observe meetings of adults.

One important theme in this section is the idea that oppressive conditions, whether intentionally enforced or not, breed superior humans or, more specifically, superior warriors. The intentionally oppressive conditions of Salusa Secundus and the naturally difficult climate of Arrakis make life on both worlds a miserable experience, but ideal for breeding potent fighters. There is a significant difference between the two worlds: the Sardaukar are bred to fight on any world, whereas the Fremen know only how to fight on Arrakis. A Fremen would be beaten if he were to meet an opponent armed with a body shield. Thus, training and technological development must go hand–in–hand with the oppressive conditions that breed tough individuals.

Paul realizes that the Fremen know only about hardship and killing. The dream that Kynes offered to them, the dream of a lush garden world, was the goal that unified and strengthened the Fremen. A new dream is replacing the dream of turning Arrakis into Eden: the dream of Paul as a savior. Paul recognizes that this dream threatens to sweep far beyond Arrakis and throw the universe into a bloody jihad. The other result of breeding such warriors is that they require some sort of glue, such as a cause to rally around or support, so that they do not give in to despair. On Salusa Secundus, the driving factor is wealth and power; on Arrakis, it is the hope of a world without strife, and after the rise of Paul, it is a dream of a universe of nothing but strife.

The idea of replacement or recycling is also important to the Fremens and Bene Gesserit, particularly as a way of preserving both the ecology of the planet, as well as the history and beliefs of the people. Water is scarce on Arrakis, so the Fremen use the water from the dead corpses to replenish their wells. When Paul kills Jamis, the Fremen remove his water and place most of it in their special wells to transform Arrakis eventually into a lush Eden. The Fremen offer some of the water to Paul, suggesting that Paul is being reborn, or reincarnated, into the Fremen clan. Because Jamis's water is recycled and shared with the world, his life force is living forever, since his water is providing life to others.

Similarly, the role of the reverend mother lives forever, even if the person in that role does not. Jessica replaces the dying woman as the reverend mother, and as a result, she gains the spirit, or life force, of all the other reverend mothers before her. The history of the Bene Gesserit people is preserved because of the reverend mothers' ability to pass down their secrets and stories from generation to generation. Even names are recycled in *Dune*: Paul calls his son Leto after his dead father, Duke Leto. Paul seeks to preserve his father's name and history, just as the Fremen people seek to preserve their land and their hope of a better future.

BOOK III (CONTINUED)

From the Fremen's discovery of smugglers to Paul's vision of a fleet of Harkonnen ships

SUMMARY
The Fremen discover and capture a melange smuggling operation in their territory. The operation is led by Gurney Halleck, Paul's old teacher and the former master-of-arms of the Atreides. Paul reveals himself to Halleck, and Halleck reaffirms his allegiance to the young duke. Paul leads Halleck and his men inside a Fremen cavern, where several of the smugglers suddenly attack since they are actually Sardaukar, the emperor's soldiers. The Fremen kill all but a few Sardaukar and they lose only a few of their own men. Paul orders the Fremen to capture the Sardaukar, but he makes plans for them to escape and report back to the Harkonnens and the emperor about the prowess of the Fremen.

Later, Paul confronts Stilgar. He observes that Stilgar's first instinct was to hide Chani when the Sardaukar attacked, showing how much he cares for Paul. Paul refuses to challenge Stilgar. Stilgar accepts Paul not as Usul of the Fremen, but as the duke of Arrakis. Stilgar's next challenge is to convince the young, headstrong Fremen that there can be both a Usul and a duke of Arrakis. That way, Paul does not lose a powerful assistant like Stilgar. Meanwhile, Halleck is shocked to discover that Paul's mother is still alive; he still believes that Paul's mother is the person who betrayed the Atreides to the Harkonnens.

Paul speaks to a large group of Fremen en masse. They try to goad him into fighting with Stilgar, but Paul resists, telling them that he is too smart to do that. Instead, Paul accepts his religious role as the Muad'Dib, the prophetic leader; he uses this role to differentiate himself from Stilgar's more secular position. Paul tells the Fremen that Rabban, the Harkonnen ruler of Arrakis, has been cut off by Baron Harkonnen from receiving any more supplies or reinforcements. Thus, Rabban does not have ties to the baron anymore, and the Fremen may be able to wrest control of Arrakis from the Harkonnens. The Fremen accept Paul's new role as duke, and they are ready to fight a fierce battle.

Paul leads his mother to his quarters, where he presents Halleck to her. Halleck quickly attacks her, believing she was the traitor to the Atreides. Holding a knife to her throat, he threatens to kill her, but Paul convinces him that she is not responsible. Halleck relents, and in his shame he tries to persuade Paul to kill him, but Paul refuses.

As Halleck plays the baliset instrument at Jessica's request, Paul goes to the place where the spice drug is made by small sandworms. He decides to drink the spice drug, as his mother did when she became the reverend mother.

Three weeks later, it appears that Paul has summoned Chani back from the south. However, it was Jessica who summoned her; Paul has been in a comalike trance for weeks. Jessica has done everything she can for him and has summoned Chani due to an inner whim. Chani realizes that Paul drank some of the spice drug and asks Jessica to quickly transform some of the drug into a safe format so that she can administer it to Paul. But at that moment, Paul wakes up, as he has changed the drug himself. He grabs Jessica's hand and demands that she show him the inward "place where you cannot enter" at which no reverend mother ever looks. Paul then speaks of two ancient forces, "one that gives and one that takes," the former being the main force of women and the latter of men—and only Paul can balance the two forces. Paul then explains that he has envisioned that there is a great fleet of ships above Arrakis, where the emperor and Baron Harkonnen and other houses wait to loot Arrakis.

ANALYSIS

The events of this section demonstrate not only that Paul is at the center of the novel's dramatic action but also that he completely controls the action. For example, Paul welcomes back his old master, Gurney Halleck, suggesting a role reversal, as if Paul is now the mentor and Halleck is the inexperienced youth. Additionally, Paul allows the Sardaukar to escape, which shows how confident he is in his own prowess and power. He feels that the Sardaukar enemies are so weak that he does not need to kill them right away. Rather, he can allow them to spread the word to the emperor about his strength and the force of the Fremen. The revelation that Paul is the Kwisatz Haderach further consolidates his potency and establishes him as a prophetic, religious leader of not just the Fremen but of the whole universe.

One way to understand Jessica's memories of previous reverend mothers is by using the theory of the "collective unconscious," or "racial memory," introduced by the psychologist Carl Jung in the first half of the twentieth century. Jung suggested that all humans share very vague, broad memories from the earliest times of human evolution, when humans lived in the same area. Jung's theory might account for why many different languages have very similar words for basic concepts such as mother and father. Jung thought that more specific memories might be passed genetically from one human to his or her offspring. This is a very broad interpretation of Jung's theories, and it is important to note that few theorists now support these ideas. In the early 1960s, however, Jung was still somewhat in vogue, and it is possible that his theories were an inspiration for Jessica's "racial memory" of her Bene Gesserit ancestors. That Jessica is much more aware of those memories than others is due to the effects of the spice drug.

Paul's ability to predict the future seems more plausible, though less realistic than Jessica's memories of reverend mothers. While it is unclear exactly how and why Paul is able to see the future whenever he consumes too much spice, it is conceivable that it is due to a heightened ability for calculation. Like a Mentat, Paul simply calculates an amazing number of variables and decides which events have the highest probability. However, this theory does not account for things that Paul could not possibly know, such as Feyd-Rautha's name or that Alia would come to be known as St. Alia of-the-Knife. In Jessica's and Paul's cases, it is probably easier to accept the idea that they have magical powers, something spiritually or supernaturally based rather than based in science. However, this detracts somewhat from *Dune*'s status as a work of science fiction and makes it more a work of fantasy.

Paul's differentiation along gender lines of the forces that give from the forces that take speaks to the intricate balance between women and men in *Dune*. Each gender is like a force in the universe, and neither has total power over the other since neither can face the other without losing something of itself. Each force, like each gender, cannot exist without the other, opposing force. Paul, however, exists above this interplay of forces. As the Kwisatz Haderach, he is the only one who can balance the logical and the intuitive, and the male and the female forces. For example, Paul can use the Voice to convince the Fremen to help fight the Sardaukar, but he must also win them over using logic. Paul's mastery of both the female and male forces means that he can become more powerful than any other human being.

BOOK III (CONTINUED)

From several ships landing on Arrakis to the end of the novel

SUMMARY

Several ships land behind Arrakis's rocky shield wall. The emperor has come to Arrakis, along with Baron Harkonnen and five legions of Sardaukar. Stilgar and Paul's plan is to wait until a great sandstorm strikes, and then break the shield wall with atomic weapons. Next, the Fremen will blast the noses off the spaceships so that the vehicles cannot take off. Then the Fremen will rush the Sardaukar, while the people of Arrakis rise up against the emperor and his forces.

When the sandstorm hits, Halleck blows up the shield wall. As Paul and his soldiers prepare for battle with the Sardaukar, they receive a message from Sietch Tabr: it has been raided, and many of its inhabitants have been killed, including Paul's son, Leto. Alia has been captured. Chani and Jessica were hiding out closer to the city, so they were not at Sietch Tabr during the raid.

Meanwhile, inside the emperor's ship, just before the shield is attacked, the baron and the emperor discuss their plans. Feyd-Rautha and Rabban are also members of the party, though they are outside the ship, scouting the perimeter. The emperor presents Alia, whom his men have captured, to the group. The emperor is enraged since only a handful of his Sardaukar got away from old men, women, and children, as the Fremen are such excellent fighters.

The emperor's truthsayer, or one who detects sincerity, is the Reverend Mother Gaius Helen Mohiam. Mohiam calls Alia an abomination—Alia has the consciousness of all reverend mothers of the past; therefore, she knows all of Mohiam's memories and is inside her mind. Just as the emperor is threatening Paul, the Fremen strike, destroying the shield wall. Alia kills the baron—who is her grandfather—with her gom jabbar and escapes. The emperor hears reports that the Fremen have breached the shields of his ships and have broken the ships' noses so they cannot lift off. Shocked, the emperor and his troops see the Fremen riding toward them on dozens of giant sandworms. The Fremen soon defeat the Sardaukar, and Paul resumes his place on the throne at the Arrakeen governor's mansion. Paul sends a Sardaukar captive as a messenger to the emperor to discuss the terms of the emperor's surrender. Paul, however, is worried: he still sees the jihad ahead of him. He now accepts the fact that he is the Kwisatz Haderach.

Chani and Jessica arrive, and then the emperor and his entourage appear. Paul asks Thufir Hawat to come forward. The baron secretly administered poisons to Hawat, and Hawat is near death. The emperor has given Hawat a poisonous needle to use to kill Paul, but Hawat refuses and dies in Paul's arms.

The emperor threatens to command the House of Landsraad ships to attack the Fremen, but Paul orders the representatives of the Spacing Guild to force the House of Landsraad ships to leave. Paul threatens that if they do not leave, Paul will destroy all the spice on Arrakis, robbing the Guildsmen of their supply. The Guildsmen obey Paul's orders, angering the emperor, who is powerless without the support of the Guild. Paul then turns his attention to the Reverend Mother Mohiam, telling her that he refuses to do the bidding of the Bene Gesserit or to be the cause of the jihad, which even the Bene Gesserit do not realize is their ultimate goal.

Feyd-Rautha challenges Paul to a duel, and Paul accepts despite his followers' protests. Feyd-Rautha cheats, as always, but he still fails and Paul kills him. The emperor tries to get Count Fenring to kill Paul, and Paul realizes that Fenring was almost a Kwisatz Haderach himself. Fenring refuses to attack Paul, which enrages the emperor. Paul then asks for the throne through a marriage to Princess Irulan, the Emperor's daughter. The emperor reluctantly agrees, and Chani negotiates the settlement. Paul assures her that while Princess Irulan will be the "royal concubine," it is Chani who will be his true wife.

ANALYSIS

Just as Paul does not know how he intends to avert the jihad, we also do not know how he plans to bring peace and not war. Herbert offers only one allusion to Paul's future plans, when Paul thinks, "They sense that I must take the throne. . . . But they cannot know I do it to prevent the jihad." As the new emperor, the most powerful person in the universe, Paul hopes to prevent the bloody deaths of millions. The idea of saving lives casts a new light on the quotations by Princess Irulan that we have read throughout the book. We do not know whether these quotations are in praise of a great religious leader who brought a time of peace or in praise of a person who has brought war. Historically, the peaceful messianic figures are remembered better than the wrathful ones. However, we still do not know whether the Fremen will become soldiers of war or guardians of peace.

Dune's final pages are filled with fast-moving action that ends abruptly. The final battle and Paul's successes are anticlimactic; we do not feel satisfied with the novel's conclusion. Without even an epilogue, it appears that Herbert intended a sequel to *Dune,* and there are eventually five sequels. The last few parts of the novel seem rushed and unfinished. The minds of Paul, Jessica, and the Reverend Mother Mohiam are filled with weighty thoughts, but none of these is resolved or explored any further, as the characters just want Paul to be enthroned as the new emperor as quickly as possible.

Paul's ascension to the emperorship and the Fremen's regaining of control complete the reversal of status that occurs during the course of the novel. At the beginning of the novel, the emperor and the Harkonnen dominated the Atreides and the Fremen. The power structure of *Dune* has changed since Paul was on Caladan. Duke Leto is dead and now Paul is not only duke of Arrakis, but also the new emperor of the universe. The Fremen have regained control of their world and will soon turn it into the garden paradise they have long desired. Once this change occurs, however, we wonder how the Fremen's culture will change—whether they will retire into easy lives of spice mining or follow their prophet into space.

Dune is still widely read and considered a landmark of science-fiction writing because it combines fantasy and science fiction with important social issues about the environment, religion, human social interaction, and genetic development. *Dune* was ahead of its time in pointing out the importance of ecological preservation and conservation of resources. Also, by addressing religion's complexity, *Dune* explored a topic that was rarely addressed by science fiction prior to the novel's publication. Today, the issues that *Dune* addresses are perhaps more relevant than they were forty years ago.

SUMMARY & ANALYSIS

IMPORTANT QUOTATIONS EXPLAINED

1.   "Religion and law among our masses must be one and
     the same," his father said. "An act of disobedience
     must be a sin and require religious penalties. This will
     have the dual benefit of bringing both greater
     obedience and greater bravery. We must depend not so
     much on the bravery of individuals, you see, as upon
     the bravery of a whole population."

Kynes's dead father says these words in Book II, when Kynes is on
the verge of death and hallucinating in the desert of Arrakis. Kynes's
father states that religion's purpose is to steer a relatively ignorant
impressionable population toward a particular goal. Kynes's father
used religion to help steer the Fremen, the indigent population of
Arrakis, a people yearning for a leader. Kynes and his father used
religion to earn the loyalty of the fierce Fremen with the purpose of
transforming Arrakis from a desert world into a green paradise. In
addition, they seek to use religion to end the crime that accompanies
the illicit trade of melange.

2.   He found that he no longer could hate the Bene
        Gesserit or the Emperor or even the Harkonnens.
        They were all caught up in the need of their race to
        renew its scattered inheritance, to cross and mingle
        and infuse their bloodlines in a great new pooling of
        genes. And the race knew only one sure way for this—
        the ancient way . . . jihad.

This passage from the end of Book I occurs when Paul and his mother, Jessica, are hiding in a tent, and she explains the forces behind what Paul calls his "terrible purpose." The Bene Gesserit, a group of women with superhuman powers, create the Kwisatz Haderach, a person who provides the "shortening of the way" toward reinvigorating humanity's stagnant gene pool. Paul realizes that the only way the human race knows how to diversify its gene pool is through bloody, fanatical warfare. The creation of a Kwisatz Haderach to help cross and mingle the bloodlines is ironic. After tens of thousands of years of technological development and human evolution, humans are still influenced first and foremost by the most primary human instinct: sex drive.

QUOTATIONS

3.   "We will treat your comrade with the same reverence
     we treat our own," the Fremen said. "This is the bond
     of water. We know the rites. A man's flesh is his own;
     the water belongs to the tribe."

In the beginning of Book II, a member of the Fremen speaks these
words to Thufir Hawat, a Mentat who served three generations of
Atreides until he reluctantly joined the Harkonnens. Hawat allows
the Fremen to take the dead body of one of his soldiers to be ren-
dered down for water. For the Fremen, water is more important
than blood. Alliances are secured with the "bond of water" rather
than with blood oaths. Fremen remove the water from a body once
it dies. They keep the water for the tribe, or they store it in wells,
where it will eventually be used to alter the climate of Arrakis.
Hawat, by allowing his own men's corpses to be tapped for precious
water, creates a strong bond between his men and the Fremen.

4.   "A duke's son must know about poisons. . . . Here's a
     new one for you: the gom jabbar. It kills only animals."

Reverend Mother Mohiam speaks these words in the beginning of
Book I. Her statement reveals the distinction the novel makes
between humans and animals. The Bene Gesserit believe that animals react only by instinct, their base emotions, and drives. They
also believe that humans can use their self-awareness to combat
instinct. A Mentat, for example, uses only logic and removes all
emotional or irrational ideas from his decision-making process.
Mother Mohiam tests whether Paul is an animal or a human being
by putting his hand in a box that causes pain. Paul passes the test by
resisting the urge to pull his hand away from the pain. He rational-
izes that he will be poisoned if he moves his hand, and thus, he fights
his instinctual drive to run from the pain. This test is the first of
many that Paul must survive to become the Kwisatz Haderach.

QUOTATIONS

5.   The drug had him again and he thought: So many times you've given me comfort and forgetfulness. He felt anew the hyperillumination with its high-relief imagery of time, sensed his future becoming memories—the tender indignities of physical love, the sharing and communion of selves, the softness and the violence.

This passage occurs in Book II after Paul takes the drug melange, which significantly changes him. His senses become more acute, and he is suddenly able to "see through time." Paul can now see infinite possibilities in future events, and he realizes his actions will cause a jihad (holy war) in the universe. Paul is also more sensitive to physical contact, particularly when he is with his love, Chani. Paul's consumption of the melange is an important turning point in his development as a Kwisatz Haderach. Paul becomes dependent on the melange to see into the future, and the addictive substance in turn begins to shackle him. Paul needs the melange to live and to fulfill his role as a Kwisatz Haderach. The French word mélange means a mixture of diverse elements. Paul's role as a Kwisatz Haderach is to mix the elements of the human gene pool—he needs melange to execute the mixture of gene pools that will ultimately save his species.

QUOTATIONS

KEY FACTS

FULL TITLE
Dune

AUTHOR
Frank Herbert

TYPE OF WORK
Novel

GENRE
Science fiction, fantasy

LANGUAGE
English

TIME AND PLACE WRITTEN
America, early 1960s

DATE OF FIRST PUBLICATION
1965

PUBLISHER
Chilton Books

NARRATOR
The third-person narrator is omniscient and anonymous. Some of the novel's main characters narrate their own feelings or emotions at different points throughout the book.

POINT OF VIEW
The narrator maintains a third-person perspective through most of the novel. The narrator is omniscient and provides insight into the thoughts and plans of certain characters while also giving clues to the novel's social, cultural, and political background. The narration sometimes switches to first-person to reveal specific characters' inner feelings and motivations.

TONE

The tone is fairly ominous and resigned. A feeling of melancholy pervades the presentation of some characters, particularly Paul. The narrator communicates an overwhelming sense that fate is immutable and that the characters are powerless to change events as they unfold.

TENSE

Immediate past, real-time narration

SETTING (TIME)

The future: 10,191

SETTING (PLACE)

Arrakis, a desert planet

PROTAGONIST

Paul Atreides

MAJOR CONFLICT

The Harkonnens, led by Baron Harkonnen, want to overthrow the emperor by taking over the melange supply on Arrakis. Paul, from the opposing house of Atreides, works with the Fremen to secure Arrakis and the universe from the greedy Harkonnens.

RISING ACTION

The Harkonnens kill Duke Leto and obliterate the Atreides. Baron Harkonnen uses the emperor's soldiers to attempt to take control of Arrakis and the melange supply while killing Kynes and Paul's son.

CLIMAX

Paul and the Fremen succeed in defeating the forces of the emperor and the Harkonnens that are invading Arrakis; Alia kills Baron Harkonnen.

FALLING ACTION

Paul arranges a marriage between himself and Princess Irulan, thus securing the imperial throne.

THEMES

Religion and power; human control over ecology

MOTIFS

Inheritance and nepotism; precognition; loyalty; fanaticism

SYMBOLS

melange; water

FORESHADOWING

Dune contains many instances of foreshadowing. Paul is
constantly foreseeing events, often long before they occur:
Paul's dream in which he is called Usul; Paul's vision of a jihad.
Also, Reverend Mother Mohiam's warning that Duke Leto will
die on Arrakis.

KEY FACTS

STUDY QUESTIONS & ESSAY TOPICS

STUDY QUESTIONS

1. *Describe Paul's relationship to the Fremen. Do they use Paul to achieve their ends, or does Paul use them?*

When Paul becomes a member of the Fremen, he has three competing priorities in his life. The first is vengeance. The Harkonnens killed Paul's father, and under the rules of kanly, Paul is required to avenge his father's death. Second, Paul shares the Fremen's desire to transform Arrakis from a desert world into a lush, Edenic paradise. Finally, Paul is compelled by a "terrible purpose" that was instilled in him by the Bene Gesserit because he is the Kwisatz Haderach. Paul's purpose, according to the beliefs of the Bene Gesserit, is to start a jihad across the universe that will promote genetic crossbreeding among human populations, since the gene pool has begun to stagnate.

Paul befriends the Fremen and manipulates them to achieve his three main goals. In the battle at the end of the novel, Paul and the Fremen kill the Harkonnens and Paul secures a position as emperor of the universe. As a result, Paul has gained revenge and the power to alter the Arrakis climate. As the leader of the universe, he can also control the jihad. While Paul embraces the dream of the Fremen to turn Arrakis into an Eden, he is also aware that the Fremen are merely the tool of other groups. For example, the Bene Gesserit used the Fremen and their belief in prophecies to protect their own people in case they were stranded. Likewise, Paul used the Fremen as a way of getting revenge on the Harkonnens and gaining control of the Imperium.

Paul is aware that the Fremen are manipulated by their religion, but he also respects their vision, and he embraces it sincerely. Paul reluctantly accepts his other goals because he has no choice: his father was murdered, and by law, he must avenge the death and follow his "terrible purpose." Paul is not obliged to help the Fremen, however. although Paul does use the power of the Fremen to achieve his ls, he helps them because he also supports their goal to make kis a lush, beautiful planet.

2.   Dune *has been referred to as "science fiction's supreme masterpiece," yet science-fiction author Arthur C. Clarke said only J. R. R. Tolkien's fantasy trilogy,* The Lord of the Rings, *could match it. Is* Dune *is a work of science fiction or a work of fantasy?*

Herbert originally published *Dune* as a serial story in the well-known science fiction magazine *Analog* in the early 1960s. Serial science fiction was part of a long tradition dating back to the early work of Clarke and Isaac Asimov in the 1930s and 1940s. *Dune*, however, represented a shift in the science-fiction genre away from concept-based writing to a form that paid more attention to plot and character. In the process, *Dune* co-opted a process formerly found in fantasy fiction known as world-building. World-building is the foundation of Tolkien's *Lord of the Rings*, and it also plays a central role in *Dune*. Like Tolkien's novels, *Dune* presents its reader with a bewildering number of imaginary people, places, things, and ideas. Herbert creates a world set 8,000 years in the future. The effect of world-building, however, is to move the story from a familiar future scenario to a more and more unrecognizable one. The progression moves the novel from the somewhat familiar sphere of speculative science fiction into a more unrecognizable world of fantasy.

Dune was one of the first major works of science fiction to blur the lines between science fiction and fantasy—two genres that are now so similar that they almost always share the same shelves at bookstores. The fantasy and science-fiction genres were combined perhaps most successfully in the *Star Wars* films, which placed fantasy tales in science fiction-influenced settings. Whereas *Star Wars* used the combination primarily for spectacle and entertainment, Herbert used *Dune*'s combination of fantasy and science fiction to address serious ecological, religious, and political issues.

3. *Discuss the role of loyalty in* Dune.

Arrakis is a desolate, harsh, dry planet, filled with smugglers and two rival houses—the Atreides and the Harkonnens—that would do anything to destroy each other. Arrakis is known for its supply of melange, an addictive drug that many people in the universe use and want to buy. The limited supply of melange has led to rampant crime and deceit on Arrakis.

The Arrakeen climate of vengeance, crime, and rivalry makes loyalty a key component of survival and peril. A breach of loyalty brings down the House of Atreides: Yueh betrays them to Baron Harkonnen. Similarly, Halleck's distrust of Jessica leads to serious trouble—he thinks that she betrayed Leto, so he tries to kill her. Both Duke Leto and Paul command fanatical devotion from their men by inspiring their loyalty and trust. Duke Leto wins loyalty through his sincere concern for the lives of his men. On the other hand, Paul, whose Fremen care little for their own lives, wins loyalty through his effective leadership and his belief in the Fremen's dream of an Edenic Arrakis.

The baron, who is loyal only to his own cause, perishes in defeat. He fails to rally the support of the Harkonnens and instead uses them to gain more power for himself. The baron is not loyal to the emperor and uses the imperial soldiers without permission. The baron is also disloyal to his family—he cuts off supplies and assistance to his nephew Rabban, allowing the Fremen to regain control of Arrakis. In the end, the baron falls victim to his failure to inspire the loyalty of his own family—his granddaughter, Alia, kills him with a knife.

Suggested Essay Topics

1. Discuss how the character of Paul Atreides changes through the course of *Dune*. Does he mature at all, or did he always act like an adult?

2. Analyze the behavior and beliefs of the Fremen. What are their morals? Are they noble freedom fighters, or simply fanatical killers?

3. How does the climate of Arrakis affect the everyday life of those who live there? What values and symbols are important on this desert planet?

4. Describe the political organization of the universe in *Dune*. Be sure to discuss the Bene Gesserit, the Imperium, the Great Houses of the Landsraad, and the Spacing Guild.

5. How does Jessica deal with her divided loyalties between the Bene Gesserit, the Atreides, and the Fremen? In the end, which is she the most loyal to and why?

QUESTIONS & ESSAYS

REVIEW & RESOURCES

QUIZ

1. What planet do the Atreides occupy at the beginning of *Dune*?

   A. Arrakis
   B. Giedi Prime
   C. Caladan
   D. Salusa Secundus

2. Which of the following defines Jessica's relationship with Duke Leto?

   A. She is his daughter
   B. She is his wife
   C. She is his sister
   D. She is his concubine

3. Jessica is a member of which of the following?

   A. Bene Gesserit
   B. Spacing Guild
   C. New York Knicks
   D. Harkonnens

4. Who betrays Duke Leto?

   A. Stilgar
   B. Dr. Yueh
   C. Jessica
   D. Duncan Idaho

5. What is Paul's tribal name among the Fremen?

   A. Stilgar
   B. Chani
   C. Usul
   D. Muad'Dib

6. What is the name of the emperor's prison planet?

    A. Salusa Secundus
    B. Corrino
    C. Arrakis
    D. Caladan

7. Which is the baron's grandson?

    A. Rabban Harkonnen
    B. Stilgar
    C. Feyd-Rautha Harkonnen
    D. Paul Atreides

8. What is the name of the Fremen garment that conserves water?

    A. Wellsuit
    B. Body shield
    C. Stillsuit
    D. Jubba cloak

9. According to the Fremen, what is a maker?

    A. A lasgun
    B. A sandworm
    C. A flask of water
    D. Someone who urinates

10. Who is the emperor's truthsayer?

    A. Count Fenring
    B. Baron Harkonnen
    C. Cotton Mather
    D. The Reverend Mother Mohiam

11. With which Fremen leader does Paul form a close relationship?

    A. Jamis
    B. Kynes
    C. Liet
    D. Stilgar

12. What is a muad'dib?

   A. A vehicle
   B. A type of desert mouse
   C. A flying tree
   D. A type of worm

13. Which one of these is a Mentat?

   A. Baron Harkonnen
   B. Thufir Hawat
   C. Duncan Idaho
   D. Gurney Halleck

14. What is the name of Paul's son?

   A. Gurney
   B. Leto
   C. Bob
   D. Usul

15. What is the name of the spice drug?

   A. Melange
   B. Gom jabber
   C. Pre-spice mass
   D. Lasgun

16. How is melange made?

   A. By rendering down the human body to its basic
      elements
   B. It is made using dew collectors
   C. It is made by the Sardaukar
   D. It is secreted by young, larval-stage sandworms

17. Who is Liet?

   A. Paul
   B. Stilgar
   C. Duke Leto
   D. Dr. Kynes

18. What is a sietch?

   A. A needle tipped with poison
   B. A Fremen cave
   C. A knife made from a worm's tooth
   D. A special robe

19. Who is Chani's father?

   A. Dr. Kynes
   B. Duke Leto
   C. The emperor
   D. Baron Harkonnen

20. What do Fremen do with their dead?

   A. Bury them in a cave
   B. Cremate them
   C. Leave them for the sandworms
   D. Render them down for their water

21. For most of the novel, who does Hawat believe betrayed the Atreides?

   A. Dr. Yueh
   B. Duncan Idaho
   C. Jessica
   D. Gurney Halleck

22. Which planet do the Atreides settle on after leaving Caladan?

   A. Earth
   B. Sietch Tabr
   C. Salusa Secundus
   D. Arrakis

23. What is the last thing Paul must do before he is accepted as a full Fremen?

   A. Ride a sandworm
   B. Kill a man with a naked blade
   C. Kill a Harkonnen
   D. Use a thumper

24. Which of the following is not one of the Great Houses of the Landsraad?

    A. The Acheans
    B. The Atreides
    C. The Corrinos
    D. The Harkonnens

25. Who is Tuek?

    A. An Atreides soldier
    B. Baron Harkonnen's Mentat
    C. A captain of the Sardaukar
    D. An Arrakeen smuggler

ANSWER KEY:
1: C; 2: D; 3: A; 4: B; 5: C; 6: A; 7: D; 8: C; 9: B; 10: D; 11:
D; 12: B; 13: B; 14: B; 15: A; 16: D; 17: D; 18: B; 19: A; 20:
D; 21: C; 22: D; 23: A; 24: A; 25: D

A Glossary of Terms Used in *Dune*

Arrakis   A desert planet and the main source of the spice-drug melange. Arrakis is controlled by the Harkonnens until it is given to Duke Leto Atreides by the emperor. Later, the Harkonnens fight to regain control of the planet. The natives of Arrakis are known as Fremen.

Baliset   A stringed instrument played by strumming. The baliset is a favorite instrument of Gurney Halleck, and Paul uses it to serenade Chani.

Bene Gesserit (B.G.) An ancient school of mental and physical training established primarily for female students. Members of the Bene Gesserit have semimystical powers, including foresight and the Voice, a special tone used to control people. The Bene Gesserit also oversee an intergalactic breeding program intended to diversity the human gene pool and keep it from becoming stagnant.

Caladan   The Earthlike planet that the Atreides inhabit at the beginning of Dune. According to the baron's agreement, the Atreides get control of Arrakis and the Harkonnen rule the planet Caladan.

Fedaykin   A squad of death commandos, or highly trained Fremen warriors, who surround Muad'Dib at all times.

Fremen   The native people of Arrakis. They are fierce warriors, as they have trained in the harsh, dry climate of their home world. They dream of transforming Arrakis into a lush, gardenlike planet. The Fremen are highly religious, and their skill in battle is superior even to that of the Sardaukar.

Gom jabbar A needlelike instrument, used by the Bene Gesserit in their test for human awareness, that can kill instantly with a special poison.

House Atreides One of the Great Houses of the Landsraad. Its leader is Duke Leto Atreides, and its members include his son, Paul, and his concubine, Jessica, Paul's mother. Their greatest rivals are the Harkonnens.

House Harkonnen One of the Great Houses of the Landsraad. House Harkonnen is led by Baron Harkonnen and includes his nephews Feyd-Rautha and Rabban. Their rival house is the Atreides.

Houses of the Landsraad The term for the great council of houses, or families, which are a third of the triangular power structure of the universe. They are balanced against the imperial household of the emperor, who nominally controls the houses, and the Guild's monopoly on space travel.

Jihad A term meaning holy war, or a war fought for religious reasons. Frank Herbert's definition of the term in the appendices to Dune is more specific: he calls a jihad a fanatical crusade.

Kanly A formal feud or vendetta. Families or houses are obliged to seek revenge for the death of one of their members. For example, Paul can seek revenge for his father's death by killing a member of the Harkonnen family.

Kwisatz Haderach A term that literally means "shortening of the way." The Bene Gesserit work toward creating a Kwisatz Haderach who will bring about the kind of changes required to keep the human gene pool from stagnating. Paul Atreides is the Kwisatz Haderach, which means he has great powers above and beyond those of the average Bene Gesserit and is capable of affecting great change across the universe.

Lasgun Laser guns. They create a subatomic explosion when used against an energy shield.

Melange The name of the spice drug that the Fremen cultivate on Arrakis. melange creates a heightened awareness in both the intellect and in the emotions of a human being. The Spacing Guild uses melange to be better pilots; Paul Atreides uses it to see into the future.

Mentat A person who is trained rigorously from birth to think and act using logic and logic alone. Mentats are not allowed to consider emotions when making decisions or thinking. Most leaders of the Great Houses of the Landsraad have at least one Mentat on their staff. Examples of Mentats are Thufir Hawat and Piter.

Missionaria Protectiva An arm of the Bene Gesserit school. Their mission is to spread legends on primitive worlds. When the civilization on that world grows, their religions will include the legends of the Bene Gesserit. Later, if a Bene Gesserit finds herself on such a world, she can exploit the legends and earn the respect of the native people.

Muad'Dib The name that the Fremen use to address Paul Atreides. It originally meant a small mouse that survives in the desert. For the Fremen, it becomes Paul's religious title and the term for their prophet.

Ornithopter A type of small flying ship that flies in the manner of a bird, with beating wings.

Reverend Mother The title for leaders, or headmasters, in the Bene Gesserit school. For the Fremen, the term is used for their religious leaders. To become a reverend mother, one must imbibe a certain poison and then take control of the body to change the poison and make it harmless.

Salusa Secundus According to common lore, Salusa Secundus is a prison planet used to punish rebels against the Empire. In truth, the emperor uses the planet as a brutal training ground to create his toughest soldiers, the Sardaukar.

Sandworms A type of worm that lives in the deserts of Arrakis and can grow up to a quarter of a mile long or more. While the sandworms pose a threat to most people on Arrakis, the Fremen have learned to ride them and use them as vehicles. The sandworms are also an important part of creating melange.

Sardaukar The soldiers of the emperor. They are trained under oppressive conditions on Salusa Secundus. The Sardaukar are said to be the best and most ruthless soldiers in the universe, armed with advanced weaponry. However, they are easily beaten by the Fremen.

Sietch A Fremen word meaning "place of assembly in time of danger." The sietches are the cave warrens where the Fremen live, and they are present all over Arrakis.

Sietch Tabr Sietch Tabr is the sietch of Stilgar, the man who inducts Paul and Jessica into the Fremen.

The Spacing Guild Like the Bene Gesserit, the Guild is a school that specializes in training people for space travel, transport, and banking. The Guild has an intergalactic monopoly on all of these activities, making it a very powerful entity.

SUGGESTIONS FOR FURTHER READING

HERBERT, FRANK. *Chapterhouse Dune*. New York: Putnam, 1985.

———. *Children of Dune*. New York: Berkley Publishing Corp., 1976.

———. *Dune Messiah*. New York: Putnam, 1969.

———. *God Emperor of Dune*. New York: G. P. Putnam's Sons, 1981.

———. *Heretics of Dune*. New York: Putnam, 1984.

———. *The Maker of* DUNE: *Insights of a Master of Science Fiction*. Timothy O'Reilly, ed. New York: Berkley Books, 1987.

———. *The Notebooks of Frank Herbert's* DUNE. Brian Herbert, ed. New York: Perigee, 1981.

LEVACK, DANIEL. DUNE *Master: a Frank Herbert Bibliography*. Westport, Connecticut: Meckler, 1988.

O'REILLY, TIMOTHY. *Frank Herbert*. New York: Ungar, 1981.

TOUPONCE, WILLIAM F. *Frank Herbert*. Boston: Twayne Publishers, 1988.

SparkNotes Study Guides: